Creating
MADE-TO-MEASURE
KNITWEAR

Creating
MADE-TO-MEASURE KNITWEAR

A REVOLUTIONARY APPROACH TO KNITWEAR DESIGN

Sylvia Wynn

GUILD OF MASTER CRAFTSMAN PUBLICATIONS

First published 2002 by
Guild of Master Craftsman Publications Ltd
Castle Place, 166 High Street,
Lewes, East Sussex BN7 1XU

Text © Sylvia Wynn 2002
© in the work GMC Publications 2002
Outdoor fashion photography © Calvey Taylor-Haw
Still life and studio photography by Anthony Bailey and the author

ISBN 1 86108 350 5

A catalogue record for this book is available from the British Library.

Editor: David Arscott
Book and cover design: Maggie Aldred

Colour origination by Universal Graphics Pte Ltd (Singapore)
Printed and bound by Printing Express Ltd., Hong Kong

ABBREVIATIONS USED IN THIS BOOK

Alt.	Alternate
Beg.	Beginning
Cm	Centimetre(s)
Dec.	Decrease
In	Inch(es)
Inc.	Increase
Inc.1	Work into front and then into back of same stitch, either knit or purl.
K	Knit
LH	Left hand
P	Purl
PSSO	Pass slipped stitch over
RH	Right hand
Rep.	Repeat
S1	Slip 1
St.	Stitch
Sts.	Stitches
St. St.	Stocking Stitch
Tbl.	Through back of loop
Tog.	Together
M1.	Make 1 stitch by bringing yarn forward and over needle, also makes a hole.
Yfon.	Yarn forward and over needle.
Up1	Increases 1 stitch. Pick up horizontal strand of yarn lying between stitch just worked and next stitch and knit into back of it.
S1, K2, PSSO and knit at same time	Could also read S1,K2,Yfon, PSSO. This is a mock cable.
e. wrap	Casting on stitches on machine by wrapping yarn around needle in shape of an e.
foll.	following
g.	gram(s)
patt.	pattern

CONTENTS

Introduction

Have you still got that hourglass figure or, like me, has the sand shifted to the bottom? Whichever is your case, my 'dimensional knitting' made-to-measure system is the answer.

The words dimensional knitting are usually associated with 3D pattern stitches, or picture knitting, but people seem to forget that our bodies are also three-dimensional. We are not 'cardboard cut-outs', but have depth – the third dimension. This is where most of our measurements take place. Our 'protruding bits' (busts, tummies and bottoms) extend in the depth of our bodies, not in the width.

Conventional patterns concentrate only on two dimensions – the width and the height – and therefore tend to increase in size all over. Accommodating the size of the bust or hips means for many of us that the shoulder is too wide and the seam hangs halfway down the arm – hence the dropped shoulder syndrome. Similarly, someone with a larger body measurement will not necessarily have

long arms. Over the years many people fluctuate in size and shape (sometimes because of dieting), and my system allows for this.

The idea of my dimensional knitting is to be able to create garments from panels which fit each part of your body. This method enables you to adjust the sizing to obtain a correct fit without having to re-knit the whole garment. The back and front panels fit across the shoulders. There are no side seams, but side panels which take into account the depth of your body – that third dimension. These can be adjusted to any size without interfering with the size of your shoulders, so producing a 'made-to-measure' garment by just taking a few simple measurements (p. 6). Each panel is in six widths and three lengths, the size range being approximately: bust/hip 36–52in; length 28–35in. These dimensions can also be increased or decreased as required (p. 7).

The panels are in plain stocking stitch, either hand- or machine-knitted (instructions are for both unless otherwise specified), and are then joined together with hand-knitted 'easy-to-do' mock cable bands. The stocking stitch panels are all begun on a few rows of waste yarn, which is finally removed so that the bottom bands can be completed in one piece with no join for the jackets or just a single join on other garments. The mock cable bands are hand-knitted, and they are worked from the top downwards.

The purpose of the bands is to join the panels together, disguise the seams and add decoration and interest to the plain panels. It is also to illustrate how well hand and machine knitting mix together, but if you wish you can hand-tool a cable or use any machine-knitted band to take up the 1½in in width.

I have also built into this system the opportunity to change styles, so that by interchanging the panels you can create various designs for jumpers, jackets, waistcoats and coats with, for example, round- or V-necks and short,

long, or cape sleeves. There are two skirt panels, one for a straight skirt and one for a gored skirt. For changing the style there are 15 panel shapes to choose from, although of course you only need four of these to make a garment.

Once you have established the correct panels for your size and shape (often referred to as your 'block'), you can create alternative designs by adding Fair Isle, textured patterns, textured yarns, lace, etc. either in the panels or the bands. You can also revert to having side seams and eliminate the two side bands and panels but still have a garment which fits correctly (p. 99). The possibilities are endless.

The best ideas are so often the simplest. What could be more basic than to accept the size we have become and tailor our clothes to fit. If you went to a professional designer that is exactly what they would do: now, by following my system, you can achieve the same result yourself.

Tension and Materials

Tensions

Tensions of hand-knitters and knitting machines vary, as do qualities and densities of yarn. Needles also vary as to their material and manufacture. Even though you may have needles made of the same material, if the manufacturer is not the same then the diameter and coating of the same size needle may be different. This will alter your tension. It is therefore essential to knit a tension square to arrive at the correct size for the garment.

The measurements in this pattern are worked to a tension of 30sts. and 40 rows to 10cms (4in). Knit a piece of stocking stitch 45 stitches by 60 rows. This should measure 15cms (6in) square when washed. This mundane exercise is well worth the effort in order to achieve a well-fitting garment.

As a guide only, for the stocking stitch we have used tension 6 + 2 dots on the Brother KH 864 standard gauge machine and size 3mm or 3.25mm needles for hand knitting depending on yarn. The hand-knitted mock cable bands have been knitted on 3mm needles unless otherwise stated. Circular needles (working backwards and forwards) will be needed for the bottom bands and cape sleeves. Sew in about 12in of band before proceeding, to check that it is not stretching or puckering the stocking stitch. If this should happen, change the size of the needles accordingly, but **do not** alter the number of rows.

Materials — *Equivalent 4 ply yarn*

There are no restrictions on the type of yarn to be used: wool, cotton, acrylic, silk, mohair mixtures, etc. It is much more interesting to experiment with different textures, and these depend largely on what type of garment is to be knitted. The machine-knitter may like to use fine industrial yarns and experiment with the weight. For instance, two strands of a fine 3-ply rather than one strand of 4-ply will make a firmer fabric, more suitable for a long coat. It is necessary, therefore, to knit to tension.

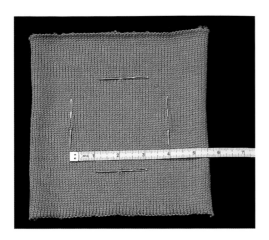

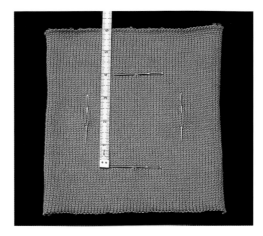

Measuring tension of knitting going across.
30sts. = 4ins.

Measuring tension of knitting going down.
40 rows = 4ins.

Machine-knitting yarns on cone can also be used for hand knitting. These are usually finer than hand-knitting yarns so do check the tension.

I personally prefer to use natural fibres, as they retain their shape and texture and there is no need for 'blocking' to size. All that is needed is a simple hand- or light machine-wash and light pressing on the wrong side. Some people are unable to wear wool and need to use man-made fibres. If this is the case, make sure that they are of a good quality: as the saying goes, 'You can't make a silk purse out of a sow's ear'.

For obvious reasons I am not able to give accurate amounts for the yarn needed – approximate guide on right.

Approximate quantities you will need for medium size in 4-ply pure new wool

JACKET:
Long length, long sleeve, 850g.
Short length, long sleeve, 650g.

JUMPER:
Short length, long sleeve, 500g.
Short length, short sleeve, 450g.

WAISTCOAT:
Short length, no sleeve, 400g.

CAPE:
Short length, cape sleeve 750g.

STRAIGHT SKIRT:
Medium length, 40g.

GORED SKIRT:
Long length, 850g.

How to Create a Garment

FOR YOUR SHAPE AND SIZE

Remember that when deciding on your measurements, a jumper to fit a size 38in bust usually measures around 41in plus. It's a good idea to measure one that you are happy with and work to that measurement.

1 Back and front panels. Measure across your shoulders, and from this measurement deduct 3in for the width of the side bands (1½in for each one). Choose the nearest size panel for the back and front. Make this a mean measurement as the mock cable bands should sit on top of the shoulders and not drop down the arm.

Example: Shoulder 14in:
Therefore: 14in-3in = 11in
See 1st size.

2 Side panels. These are determined by your bust and hip measurements. Measure your bust, allowing an extra 3in approx. for movement and sewing up. Deduct from this the total shoulder measurement times two, then divide this figure by two. This will give you a measurement for each side panel.

Example: Bust 39in:
39in + 3in = 42in
Shoulder 14in:
14in x 2 = 28in,
Therefore: 42in - 28in =
14in divided by 2 = 7in
See 3rd size.

Measure your hip following instructions as for bust.
If you require the top with straight side panels and your hip measurement is the same as your bust measurement, then choose the same size panel as you have chosen when measuring your bust.
If, however, your hip measurement is larger than your bust measurement you will obviously need to choose the larger size side panel, but this will give you a loose-fitting bust.
If, as is possible, there is too great a difference I would suggest that you use the flared side panel.

Example: Hip 42in:

> 42in + 3in = 45in
>
> Shoulder 14in:
>
> 14in x 2 = 28in
>
> Therefore: 45in - 28in =
>
> 17in divided by 2 = 8.5in
>
> See 6th size.

In this instance, rather than have the bust 3in larger than needed, I would recommend working the 3rd size flared side panel. If you are making a three-quarter or long jacket you will need to work the flared side panel to give extra room around the bottom.

3 Sleeves. Always work the sleeve panels the same size as the side panels, otherwise the armholes will not fit together correctly. The sleeves can be lengthened or shortened where indicated on the pattern. Alternatively, to add more rows to the length, increase the number of decreasings every 6th row and decrease (by the same amount) the number of decreasings every 4th row. This will give you an extra 2 rows each time. To shorten the length, work in reverse.

4 Length. There are three different lengths, the measurements of which are given in the pattern. Most of these are adjustable by multiples of four rows, which is the number of pattern rows in the mock cable. Remember that you will need to alter the distance between the buttonholes if you choose to use your own measurements for a button-through jacket.

Example: If you reduce the length by 28 rows (2.8in) you will need to work one less cable pattern (= 4 rows) between each buttonhole. This would give you a finished length of 25½in including the band.

5 Width. I have endeavoured to include most sizes in this pattern book, but you may wish to alter the width either more or less than the sizes given. The width is adjustable in multiples of six stitches, apart from jacket fronts and side panels for square armholes, which can be in multiples of three stitches. This is to accommodate the mock cable bands on the bottom of the garments.

6 Short-sleeve jumper. This may need a narrower armhole and sleeve than a jacket, in which case work four rows fewer on the back and front (in between armhole and shoulder) and six stitches fewer on the width of the sleeves.

7 **The short-length jackets** are button-through with nine buttonholes, and the medium and long-length jackets have five buttonholes for the round neck version and four buttonholes for the V-neck version.

8 **Cape.** Work the side panels for the sleeveless top either straight or flared, and work the cable band on top of the side panel.

9 **Armholes.** There are three types of armholes:

Square: (Side panels pp. 28–38; sleeves pp. 42–46) This is for a set-in sleeve, where the straight part without shaping, at the top of the sleeve, is joined to the cast-off edge of the side panel. It is recommended that you begin with this type of armhole when ascertaining your correct fit.

Shaped armholes for sleeveless top: These are curved for sleeveless garments (pp. 30 and 40).

Shaped armholes for tops with sleeves: (Side panels p. 54–56; sleeves pp. 57–63)

Finishing

Jacket with round neckline, straight side panels and sleeves with square armhole.

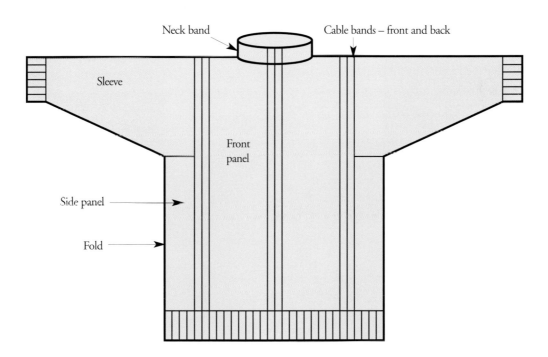

Neck band — Cable bands – front and back

Sleeve

Front panel

Side panel

Fold

It is advisable to make and finish the garment before washing or pressing. Press stocking stitch panels on wrong side, omitting mock cable bands. If necessary, steam bands only (not press) and gently pull into shape. All vertical joins are made with mattress stitch row for row (instructions p. 12) except for the armholes.

Jumper
- Sew mock cable side bands to back and front.
- Sew side panels to cable bands.
- Fit sleeves:

Straight armholes. Mark centre of sleeve and pin to shoulder seam. Sew cast-on edge of sleeve to remaining side bands on back and front. Sew straight edge at top of sleeve to top of side panels as far as marker, then join together the remaining sleeve seam, including cuff.

Shaped armholes. Starting at top of armhole shaping on sleeve and side panel, join down to cast-off edges of side panel and sleeve. Join sleeve seam, including cuff. Graft cast-off edges of armhole together. Mark centre of sleeve and pin to shoulder seam. Join top of sleeve to remaining side bands on back and front.

Jacket

• Sew mock cable side bands to back and fronts.
• Sew side panels to cable bands.
• Sew in button and buttonhole bands and attach buttons accordingly.
• Sew in sleeves as for jumper.
• Sew in all loose ends.

Shaped armhole

Straight armhole

Cape: short length, with round neckline, straight side panels for sleeveless top and cape sleeves.
Alternative design: long length, with round neckline, flared side panels for sleeveless top and cape
sleeves. (See p. 49.)

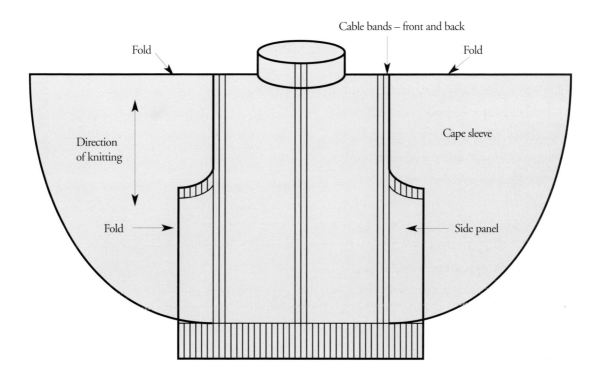

Cape

Sew mock cable side bands to back
and fronts with mattress stitch, row for
row. Sew on button and buttonhole
bands and attach buttons accordingly.
Divide cape sleeves in half and pin
centre marker to shoulder seam.
Starting at top, join cape sleeves to
cable side bands with mattress stitch,
row for row.

For long length, starting at bottom
edge, join side panels to cable side
bands with mattress stitch, row for
row, up to cape sleeve edge.
For both lengths, attach remaining
side panels to back of side bands
underneath the cape sleeves.
Fasten down cable band on cape
sleeve.
Sew in all loose ends.

Finishing stitches

My mother always said that 'If a thing's worth doing, it's worth doing well'. Many people learn how to knit but never seem to attach the same enthusiasm to the finishing of a garment. This is usually because they have not learnt two simple techniques: **Grafting**, for joining horizontally, and **Mattress Stitch**, for joining vertically. These are methods of invisible seaming and may take a little time to get used to initially, but it is well worth the effort to achieve a professional finish.

Mattress stitch

Thread a tapestry needle with the appropriate yarn. I usually work one stitch in from the edge of the knitting, but if using double knitting or chunky yarn then half a stitch would be sufficient.

With the right sides of work facing and the bottom edges level, place the sewing needle (through to the back) in between the last two stitches in the first row on the right-hand piece of work, and bring it up again in the second row (through to the front), thus picking up the bar between the stitches. Then place the needle under the strand of yarn between the first two stitches in the first row on the

left-hand piece of work and bring it up again. Repeat this in the second row and so on.

Work the mattress stitch loosely row for row for about a dozen rows and then pull up firmly to form an invisible seam. Stretch the seam slightly to give some elasticity. Continue until the seam is completed. Sometimes it is only necessary to work over two rows if preferred.

Mattress stitch

Grafting

Off the needles This can also be done over the cast-off edges if you don't want to take it off the needles. We usually do this because it gives the shoulders a firm neat finish.

Lay the pieces of work to be joined, right side up, close together with the

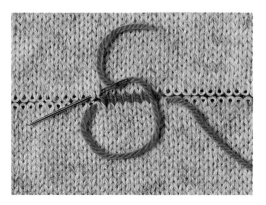

Grafting: Fig 1

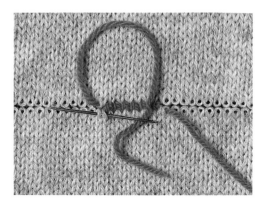

Grafting: Fig 2

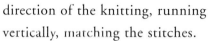

direction of the knitting, running vertically, matching the stitches.

Working right to left, bring the needle up through the first stitch of the lower piece and down through the first stitch on the upper piece, then up through the second stitch of the upper piece. (fig 1) Down through the first stitch on the lower piece then up through the second stitch of the lower piece (fig 2). Down through the second stitch of the upper piece; and then up through the third stitch of the upper piece and down through the second stitch of the lower piece. Continue until seam is completed. This is very similar to Swiss darning.

On the needles. Thread needle with a length of knitting yarn. Place the two pieces to be joined with wrong sides together and right side facing, and hold the knitting needles in your left hand.

* Pass the wool needle knitwise through the first stitch on the front needle and slip the stitch off the knitting needle. Pass the wool needle purlwise through the second stitch on the same needle, leaving the stitch on the needle.

Pass purlwise through the first stitch on the back knitting needle and slip the stitch off, then pass knitwise through the second stitch on the same needle, leaving the stitch on the needle. Repeat from * to end.

This row you have just made may become uneven at first and you may need to pull the yarn you have been working with through the work until you have the same tension as the rest of the knitting.

Back panel

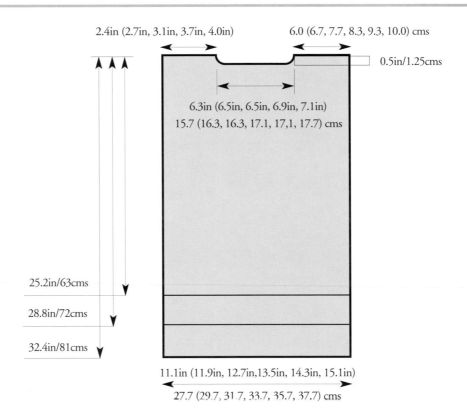

2.4in (2.7in, 3.1in, 3.7in, 4.0in)   6.0 (6.7, 7.7, 8.3, 9.3, 10.0) cms

0.5in/1.25cms

6.3in (6.5in, 6.5in, 6.9in, 7.1in)
15.7 (16.3, 16.3, 17.1, 17,1, 17.7) cms

25.2in/63cms

28.8in/72cms

32.4in/81cms

11.1in (11.9in, 12.7in,13.5in, 14.3in, 15.1in)
27.7 (29.7, 31.7, 33.7, 35.7, 37.7) cms

Back panel *(Use for all top garments)*

With waste yarn cast on 83 (89; 95; 101; 107; 113) sts. and work 4 rows
in stocking stitch.

With main yarn work 247 rows in stocking stitch for short length, 283 rows for
medium length and 319 rows for long length.

Neck shaping

Work 20 (22; 25; 27; 30; 32)sts. and leave remaining stitches on hold position for
machine or turn for hand knitting.

*Decrease 1 stitch at neck edge on next row. Work 1 row.

Rep. from * once. Cast off 18 (20; 23; 25; 28; 30) sts.

(252 rows for short length, 288 rows for medium length and 324 rows for long length)

Rejoin yarn to remaining 63 (67; 70; 74; 77; 81) sts. and continue as follows:

Cast off 43 (45; 45; 47; 47; 49) sts. for back neck and work across remaining 20 (22; 25; 27; 30; 32) sts.

*Decrease 1 stitch at neck edge on next row. Work 1 row.

Rep. from * once.

Cast off 18 (20; 23; 25; 28; 30) sts.

(252 rows for short length, 288 rows for medium length and 324 rows for long length) Remove waste yarn and place first row of main yarn on to holder.

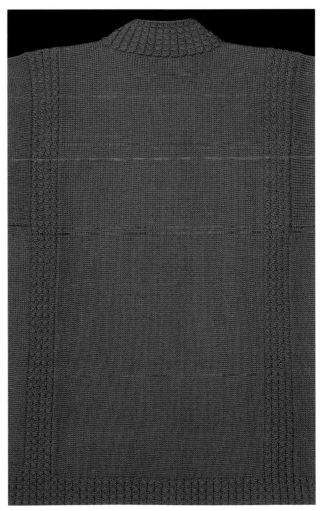

Back panel

Front Panel

FOR ROUND-NECK JUMPER, TUNIC OR DRESS

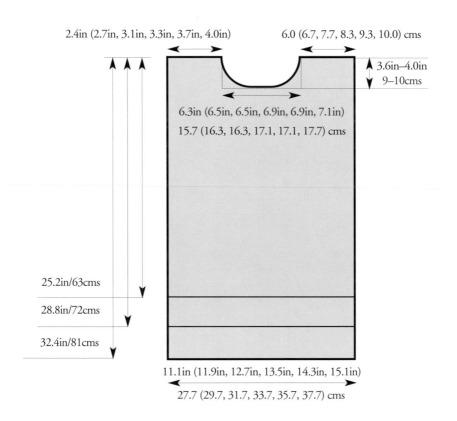

2.4in (2.7in, 3.1in, 3.3in, 3.7in, 4.0in)

6.0 (6.7, 7.7, 8.3, 9.3, 10.0) cms

3.6in–4.0in
9–10cms

6.3in (6.5in, 6.5in, 6.9in, 6.9in, 7.1in)
15.7 (16.3, 16.3, 17.1, 17.1, 17.7) cms

25.2in/63cms

28.8in/72cms

32.4in/81cms

11.1in (11.9in, 12.7in, 13.5in, 14.3in, 15.1in)
27.7 (29.7, 31.7, 33.7, 35.7, 37.7) cms

Front panel *(Round neckline)*

With waste yarn cast on 83 (89; 95; 101; 107; 113)sts. and work 4 rows in stocking stitch.

If hand knitting start with purl row.

With main yarn work 216 (214; 214; 214; 214; 212) rows in

Pictured opposite:
Round-neck
jumper; straight
side panels; short
sleeves.

stocking stitch for short length, 252 (250; 250; 250; 250; 248) rows for medium length and 288 (286; 286; 286; 286; 284) rows for long length.

Neck shaping

Work across 32 (34; 37; 39; 42; 44) sts. and leave remaining 51 (55; 58; 62; 65; 69)sts. on hold position for machine knitting or holder for hand knitting.

*Decrease 1 stitch at neck edge on next 6 rows. 26 (28; 31; 33; 36; 38)sts.

Decrease 1 stitch at neck edge on next and every alt. row until 18 (20; 23; 25; 28; 30) sts. remain.

Work 14 (16; 16; 16; 16; 18) rows of stocking stitch without shaping. Cast off. **

Rejoin yarn to remaining 51 (55; 58; 62; 65; 69) sts. and continue as follows:

Cast off 19 (21; 21; 23; 23; 25) sts. and work across remaining 32 (34; 37; 39; 42; 44)sts.

Rep. from * to **.

(252 rows for short length, 288 rows for medium length and 324 rows for long length).

Remove waste yarn and place first row of main yarn on to holder.

Front panel for round-neck jumper.

Front Panels

FOR ROUND-NECK JACKET/WAISTCOAT

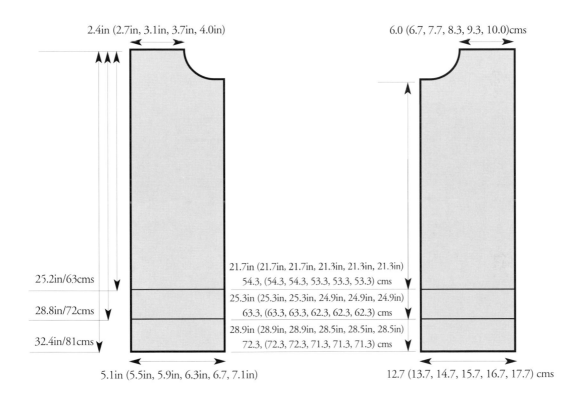

2.4in (2.7in, 3.1in, 3.7in, 4.0in)

6.0 (6.7, 7.7, 8.3, 9.3, 10.0)cms

25.2in/63cms

28.8in/72cms

32.4in/81cms

21.7in (21.7in, 21.7in, 21.3in, 21.3in, 21.3in)
54.3, (54.3, 54.3, 53.3, 53.3, 53.3) cms

25.3in (25.3in, 25.3in, 24.9in, 24.9in, 24.9in)
63.3, (63.3, 63.3, 62.3, 62.3, 62.3) cms

28.9in (28.9in, 28.9in, 28.5in, 28.5in, 28.5in)
72.3, (72.3, 72.3, 71.3, 71.3, 71.3) cms

5.1in (5.5in, 5.9in, 6.3in, 6.7, 7.1in)

12.7 (13.7, 14.7, 15.7, 16.7, 17.7) cms

Work 2 pieces, reversing shapings. If machine knitting start right front with carriage on right and left front with carriage on left. If hand knitting start right front with a purl row and left front with a knit row.

With waste yarn cast on 38 (41; 44; 47; 50; 53) sts. and work 4 rows in stocking stitch.

With main yarn work 217 (217; 217; 213; 213; 213) rows in stocking stitch for short length, 253 (253; 253; 249; 249; 249) rows for medium length and 289 (289; 289; 285; 285; 285) rows for long length.

Neck shaping

Cast off 3 (4; 5; 4; 5; 6) sts. at neck edge on next row. 35 (37; 39; 43; 45; 47) sts.

Decrease 1 stitch at neck edge on next 8 rows. 27 (29; 31; 35; 37; 39) sts.

Decrease 1 stitch at neck edge on next and every alt. row until 18 (20; 23; 25; 28; 30) sts. remain.

Work 9 (9; 11; 11; 13; 13) rows without shaping (252 rows for short length, 288 rows for medium length and 324 rows for long length) Cast off.

Remove waste yarn and place first row of main yarn on to holder.

Pictured left: Round-neck jacket panels.
Pictured on the opposite page: Suit: round-neck jacket with straight side panels; long sleeves; short length; straight skirt.

Front Panel

FOR V-NECK JUMPER, TUNIC OR DRESS

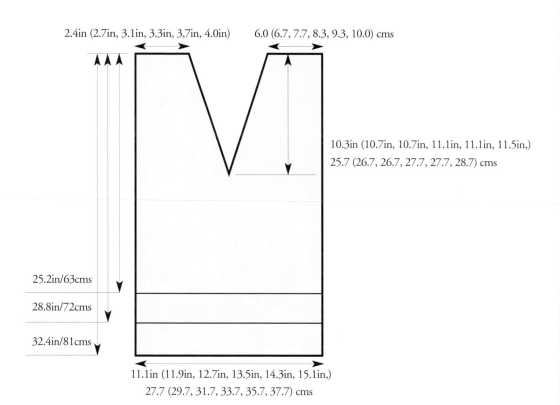

2.4in (2.7in, 3.1in, 3.3in, 3,7in, 4.0in)

6.0 (6.7, 7.7, 8.3, 9.3, 10.0) cms

10.3in (10.7in, 10.7in, 11.1in, 11.1in, 11.5in,)
25.7 (26.7, 26.7, 27.7, 27.7, 28.7) cms

25.2in/63cms

28.8in/72cms

32.4in/81cms

11.1in (11.9in, 12.7in, 13.5in, 14.3in, 15.1in,)
27.7 (29.7, 31.7, 33.7, 35.7, 37.7) cms

Front panel *(V Neckline)*

With waste yarn cast on 83 (89; 95; 101; 107; 113) sts. and work 3 rows in stocking stitch.

With main yarn, begin with purl row if hand knitting and carriage on right if machine knitting. Work 149 (145; 145; 141; 141; 137) rows in st. st. for short length, 185 (181; 181;

Pictured opposite:
V-neck jumper;
straight side panels;
long sleeves.

177; 177; 173) rows for medium length, and 221 (217; 217; 213; 213; 209) rows for long length.

V-Neck shaping

Method of decreasing

Hand knit   Decrease on right front as follows: K1, K2 tog., knit to end.

Decrease on left front as follows: Knit to last 3 sts. S1, K1, PSSO, K1.

Machine knit Decrease on right front as follows: Using 2-hole transfer hook take end 2 stitches on left side of work and move them 1 stitch to right so that decrease is worked on 2nd stitch from the edge.

Decrease on left front as follows: Using 2-hole transfer hook take end 2 stitches on right side of work and move 1 stitch to left so that decrease is worked on 2nd stitch from the edge.

Next Row Work across 41 (44; 47; 50; 53; 56) sts., leave remaining sts. on hold position for machine knitting and holder for hand knitting.

Work 3 rows on first 41 (44; 47; 50; 53; 56) sts., for left-hand side of neck.

Next Row Decrease 1 stitch on neck edge on next and every following 4th row until 18 (20; 23; 25; 28; 30) stitches remain.

Work 10 rows without shaping. Cast off. Leave centre stitch on holder, rejoin yarn to remaining stitches and work to end. Continue right side to match (252 rows for short length, 288 rows for medium length and 324 rows for long length). Remove waste yarn and place first row of main yarn on to holder.

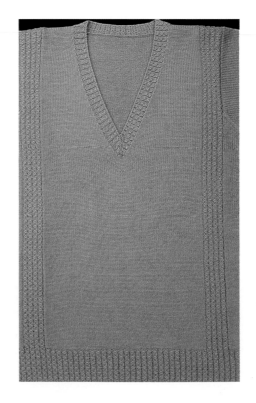

Front panel of V neck jumper.

Front Panels

V-NECK JACKET/WAISTCOAT

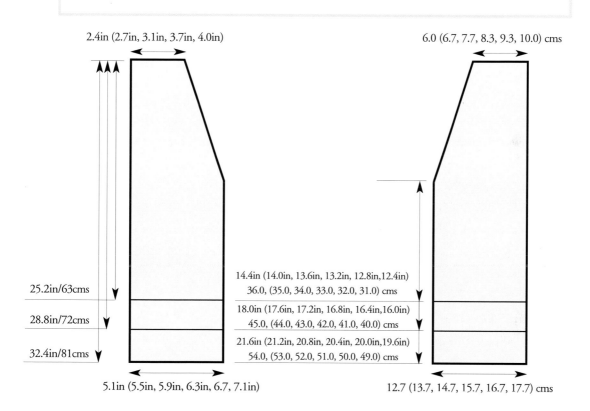

2.4in (2.7in, 3.1in, 3.7in, 4.0in)

6.0 (6.7, 7.7, 8.3, 9.3, 10.0) cms

14.4in (14.0in, 13.6in, 13.2in, 12.8in, 12.4in)
36.0, (35.0, 34.0, 33.0, 32.0, 31.0) cms

18.0in (17.6in, 17.2in, 16.8in, 16.4in, 16.0in)
45.0, (44.0, 43.0, 42.0, 41.0, 40.0) cms

21.6in (21.2in, 20.8in, 20.4in, 20.0in, 19.6in)
54.0, (53.0, 52.0, 51.0, 50.0, 49.0) cms

25.2in/63cms

28.8in/72cms

32.4in/81cms

5.1in (5.5in, 5.9in, 6.3in, 6.7, 7.1in)

12.7 (13.7, 14.7, 15.7, 16.7, 17.7) cms

Work 2 pieces, reversing shapings.

Note * for V-neck shaping

Hand Knit: Decrease on right front as follows:

> **Knit Row** K1, K2 tog., knit to end.
> **Purl Row** Purl to last 3sts., P2 tog., P1.
> Decrease on left front as follows:
> **Knit Row** Knit to last 3sts., S1, K1, PSSO, K1.
> **Purl Row** P1, P2 tog. tbl., purl to end.

Overleaf:
Suit: V-neck jacket;
round-neck jumper;
straight skirt.

25

Machine Knit Decrease on right front as follows: Using 2-hole transfer hook take end two stitches on left side of work and move them one stitch to right so that decrease is worked on 2nd stitch from the edge.

Decrease on left front as follows: Using 2-hole transfer hook take end two stitches on right side of work and move one stitch to left so that decrease is worked on 2nd stitch from the edge.

With waste yarn cast on 38 (41; 44; 47; 50; 53) sts. and work 4 rows in stocking stitch. If hand knitting start with a knit row.

With main yarn work 144 (140; 136; 132; 128; 124) rows in stocking stitch for short length, 180 (176; 172; 168; 164; 160) rows for medium length and 216 (212; 208; 204; 200; 196) rows for long length.

V-Neck shaping (see notes on Hand Knit, previous page, and Machine Knit, above)

First Size Decrease at front edge (see note *) on next then every following 6th row 4 more times (33sts.) then every 5th row 15 times (18sts.). Work 8 rows without shaping.

Second Size Decrease at front edge (see note*) on next then every following 6th row 4 more times (36sts.) then every 5th row 16 times (20sts.). Work 7 rows without shaping.

Third Size Decrease at front edge (see note*) on next then every following 6th row 6 more times (37sts.) then every 5th row 14 times (23sts.). Work 9 rows without shaping.

Fourth Size Decrease at front edge (see note*) on next then every following 6th row 6 more times (40sts.) then every 5th row 15 times (25sts.). Work 8 rows without shaping.

Fifth Size Decrease at front edge (see note*) on next then every following 6th row 8 more times (41sts.) then every 5th row 13 times (28sts.). Work 10 rows without shaping.

Sixth Size Decrease at front edge (see note*) on next then every following 6th row 7 more times (45sts.) then every 5th row 15 times (30sts.). Work 10 rows without shaping.

(252 rows for short length, 288 rows for medium length and 324 rows for long length)

Cast off. Remove waste yarn and place first row of main yarn on to holder.

Straight Side Panels

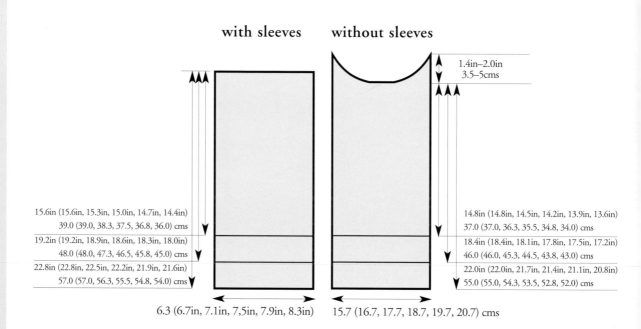

with sleeves   without sleeves

1.4in–2.0in
3.5–5cms

15.6in (15.6in, 15.3in, 15.0in, 14.7in, 14.4in)
39.0 (39.0, 38.3, 37.5, 36.8, 36.0) cms
19.2in (19.2in, 18.9in, 18.6in, 18.3in, 18.0in)
48.0 (48.0, 47.3, 46.5, 45.8, 45.0) cms
22.8in (22.8in, 22.5in, 22.2in, 21.9in, 21.6in)
57.0 (57.0, 56.3, 55.5, 54.8, 54.0) cms

14.8in (14.8in, 14.5in, 14.2in, 13.9in, 13.6in)
37.0 (37.0, 36.3, 35.5, 34.8, 34.0) cms
18.4in (18.4in, 18.1in, 17.8in, 17.5in, 17.2in)
46.0 (46.0, 45.3, 44.5, 43.8, 43.0) cms
22.0in (22.0in, 21.7in, 21.4in, 21.1in, 20.8in)
55.0 (55.0, 54.3, 53.5, 52.8, 52.0) cms

6.3 (6.7in, 7.1in, 7,5in, 7.9in, 8.3in)   15.7 (16.7, 17.7, 18.7, 19.7, 20.7) cms

Straight side panel for top with sleeves

Square armhole (Sleeves pp. 42–46)

With waste yarn cast on 47 (50; 53; 56; 59; 62) sts. and work
4 rows in stocking stitch.

With main yarn work 156 (156; 153; 150; 147; 144) rows in
stocking stitch for short length, 192 (192; 189; 186; 183;
180) rows for medium length, and 228 (228; 225; 222; 219;
216) rows for long length.

Cast off.

Remove waste yarn and place first row of main yarn on to holder.

*Pictured on
opposite page:
Dress: Round-neck;
straight side panels;
long sleeves;
long length.*

Straight side panel for sleeveless top

With waste yarn cast on 47 (50; 53; 56; 59; 62) sts. and work 4 rows in stocking stitch.

With main yarn work 148 (148; 145; 142; 139; 136) rows in stocking stitch for short length, 184 (184; 181; 178; 175; 172) rows for medium length, and 220 (220; 217; 214; 211; 208) rows for long length.

Shape armhole

Work 14 (15; 16; 17; 18; 19) sts. and leave remaining 33 (35; 37; 39; 41; 43) sts. on hold position for machine knitting or turn for hand knitting.

Straight side panel for top with sleeves (see p. 28).

Next Row Work 2 tog., work 12 (13; 14; 15; 16; 17) sts.

Next Row Work 11 (12; 13; 14; 15; 16) sts. Work 2 tog.

Continue decreasing on every row until 1 stitch remains, cast off.

Rejoin yarn to remaining stitches, cast off 19 (20; 21; 22; 23; 24) sts. and work to end.

Next Row Work 12 (13; 14; 15; 16; 17) sts. Work 2 tog.

Next Row Work 2 tog., work 11 (12; 13; 14; 15; 16) sts.

Continue decreasing on every row until 1 stitch remains, cast off.

162 (163; 161; 159; 157; 155) rows for short length, 198 (199; 197; 195; 193; 191) rows for medium length, 234 (235; 233; 231; 229; 227) rows for long length.

Remove waste yarn and place first row of main yarn on to holder.

Flared Side Panel

FOR TOP WITH SLEEVES

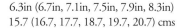

6.3in (6.7in, 7.1in, 7.5in, 7.9in, 8.3in)
15.7 (16.7, 17.7, 18.7, 19.7, 20.7) cms

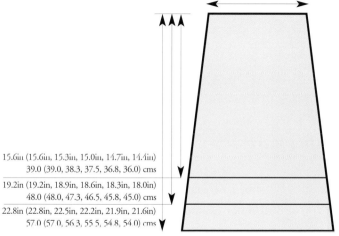

Bottom width

15.6in (15.6in, 15.3in, 15.0in, 14.7in, 14.4in)
39.0 (39.0, 38.3, 37.5, 36.8, 36.0) cms

9.5in (9.9in, 10.3in, 10.7in, 11.1in, 11.5in)
23.7 (24.7, 25.7, 26.7, 27.7, 28.7) cms

19.2in (19.2in, 18.9in, 18.6in, 18.3in, 18.0in)
48.0 (48.0, 47.3, 46.5, 45.8, 45.0) cms

10.3in (10.7in, 11.1in, 11.5in, 11.9in, 12.3in)
25.7 (26.7, 27.7, 28.7, 29.7, 30.7) cms

22.8in (22.8in, 22.5in, 22.2in, 21.9in, 21.6in)
57.0 (57.0, 56.3, 55.5, 54.8, 54.0) cms

11.1in (11.5in, 11.9in, 12.3in, 12.7in, 13.1in)
27.7 (28.7, 29.7, 30.7, 31.7, 32.7)cms

(For sleeves with square armhole, see p. 42)

Short length – Machine knit

Abbreviations

1L = First needle to the left of centre of needle bed.

1R = First needle to the right of centre of needle bed.

Row A Decrease 1 stitch by transferring stitch from needle 1L on to needle 1R then move all stitches on left of centre 1 needle to the right.

Row B Decrease 1 stitch by transferring stitch from needle 1R on to needle 1L then move all stitches on right of centre 1 needle to the left.

Push 71 (74; 77; 80; 83; 86) needles forward to working position in centre of needle bed. Extra stitch on left for odd number of stitches, even number of stitches centred equally.

With carriage on right and waste yarn, cast on and work 4 rows ending with carriage on right.

Set row counter to 000. Using main yarn, work 6 rows in stocking stitch.

Next Row Work Row A. Work 5 rows in stocking stitch.

Next Row Work Row B. Work 5 rows in stocking stitch.

Repeat last 12 rows 9 times.

Next Row Work Row A. Work 5 rows in stocking stitch.

Next Row Work Row B. 49 (52; 55; 58; 61; 64) sts. 133 rows.***

Work 5 Rows in stocking stitch.

Next Row Work Row A. 48 (51; 54; 57; 60; 63) sts. 144 rows.

Work a further 17 (17; 14; 11; 8; 5) rows. 156 (156; 153; 150; 147; 144) rows in all. Cast off. Remove waste yarn and place first row of main yarn on to holder.

Medium length – Machine knit

Abbreviations see short length page 31

Push 77 (80; 83; 86; 89; 92) needles forward to working position in centre of needle bed. Extra stitch on left for odd number of stitches, even number of stitches centred equally.

With carriage on right and waste yarn cast on and work 4 rows ending with carriage on right.

Set row counter to 000. Using main yarn, work 6 rows.

Next Row Work Row A. Work 5 rows in stocking stitch.

Next Row Work Row B. Work 5 rows in stocking stitch.

Repeat last 12 rows 12 times.

Next Row Work Row A. Work 5 rows in stocking stitch.

Next Row Work Row B. 49 (52; 55; 58; 61; 64) sts. 169 rows.***

Pictured opposite: Suit with round-necked jacket: flared side panels; long length; long sleeves; straight skirt.

Work 5 Rows in stocking stitch.

Next Row Work Row A. 48 (51; 54; 57; 60; 63) sts. 175 rows.

Work 17 (17; 14; 11; 8; 5) rows in stocking stitch. 192 (192; 189; 186; 183; 180) rows in all.

Cast off. Remove waste yarn and place first row of main yarn on to holder.

Long length – Machine knit

Abbreviations see short length page 31

Push 83 (86; 89; 92; 95; 98) needles forward to working position in centre of needle bed. Extra stitch on left for odd number of stitches, even number of stitches centred equally.

With carriage on right and waste yarn cast on and work 4 rows ending with carriage on right. Set row counter to 000.

Using main yarn, work 6 rows.

Next Row Work Row A. Work 5 rows in stocking stitch.

Next Row Work Row B. Work 5 rows in stocking stitch.

Repeat the last 12 rows 15 times.

Next Row Work Row A. Work 5 rows in stocking stitch.

Next Row Work Row B. 49 (52; 55; 58; 61; 64) sts. 205 rows. ***

Work 5 rows in stocking stitch.

Next Row Work Row A.

48 (51; 54; 57; 60; 63) sts. 211 rows.

Work 17 (17; 14; 11; 8; 5) rows in stocking stitch. 228 (228; 225; 222; 219; 216) rows in all.

Cast off. Remove waste yarn and place first row of main yarn on to holder.

Flared side panel with sleeve.

Short length – Hand knit

With waste yarn cast on 71 (74; 77; 80; 83; 86) sts. and work 4 rows in stocking stitch. With main yarn work 6 rows in stocking stitch.

Next Row K34 (36; 37; 39; 40; 42), K2 tog., K35 (36; 38; 39; 41; 42)

Stocking stitch 5 rows.

Next Row K34 (35; 37; 38; 40; 41), S1, K1, PSSO, K34 (36; 37; 39; 40; 42)

Continue decreasing as follows, working 5 rows in between each decrease row.

Next Row K33 (35; 36; 38; 39; 41). K2 tog., K34 (35; 37; 38; 40; 41)

Next Row K33 (34; 36; 37; 39; 40), S1, K1, PSSO, K33 (35; 36; 38; 39; 41)

Next Row K32 (34; 35; 37; 38; 40), K2 tog., K33 (34; 36; 37; 39; 40)

Next Row K32 (33; 35; 36; 38; 39), S1, K1, PSSO, K32 (34; 35; 37; 38; 40)

Next Row K31 (33; 34; 36; 37; 39), K2 tog., K32 (33; 35; 36; 38; 39)

Next Row K31 (32; 34; 35; 37; 38), S1, K1, PSSO, K31 (33; 34; 36; 37; 39)

Next Row K30 (32; 33; 35; 36; 38), K2 tog., K31 (32; 34; 35; 37; 38)

Next Row K30 (31; 33; 34; 36; 37), S1, K1, PSSO, K30 (32; 33; 35; 36; 38)

Next Row K29 (31; 32; 34; 35; 37). K2 tog., K30 (31; 33; 34; 36; 37)

Next Row K29 (30; 32; 33; 35; 36), S1, K1, PSSO, K29 (31; 32; 34; 35; 37)

Next Row K28 (30; 31; 33; 34; 36), K2 tog., K29 (30; 32; 33; 35; 36)

Next Row K28 (29; 31; 32; 34; 35), S1, K1, PSSO, K28 (30; 31; 33; 34; 36)

Next Row K27 (29; 30; 32; 33; 35). K2 tog. K28 (29; 31; 32; 34; 35)

Next Row K27 (28; 30; 31; 33; 34), S1, K1, PSSO, K27 (29; 30; 32; 33; 35)

Next Row K26 (28; 29; 31; 32; 34), K2 tog., K27 (28; 30; 31; 33; 34)

Next Row K26 (27; 29; 30; 32; 33), S1, K1, PSSO, K26 (28; 29; 31; 32; 34)

Next Row K25 (27; 28; 30; 31; 33),. K2 tog., K26 (27; 29; 30; 32; 33)

Next Row K25 (26; 28; 29; 31; 32), S1, K1, PSSO, K25 (27; 28; 30; 31; 33)

Next Row K24 (26; 27; 29; 30; 32), K2 tog. ,K25 (26; 28; 29; 31; 32)

Next Row K24 (25; 27; 28; 30; 31), S1, K1, PSSO, K24 (26; 27; 29; 30; 32)

49 (52; 55; 58; 61; 64) sts. (22 decrease rows) 133 rows.***

Stocking stitch 5 rows.

Next Row K23 (25; 26; 28; 29; 31), K2 tog., K24 (25; 27; 28; 30; 31).

48 (51; 54; 57; 60; 63) sts. 144 rows.

Stocking stitch 17 (17; 14; 11; 8; 5) rows. 156 (156; 153; 150; 147; 144) rows.

Cast off. Remove waste yarn and place first row of main yarn on to holder.

Medium length – Hand knit

With waste yarn cast on 77 (80; 83; 86; 89; 92) sts. and work 4 rows in stocking stitch. With main yarn work 6 rows in stocking stitch.

Next Row K37 (39; 40; 42; 43; 45) K2 tog. K38 (39; 41; 42; 44; 45)

Stocking Stitch 5 rows.

Next Row K37 (38; 40; 41; 43; 44), S1, K1, PSSO, K37 (39; 40; 42; 43; 45)

Continue decreasing as follows, working 5 rows in between each decrease row.

Next Row K36 (38; 39; 41; 42; 44), K2 tog., K37 (38; 40; 41; 43; 44)

Next Row K36 (37; 39; 40; 42; 43), S1, K1, PSSO, K36 (38; 39; 41; 42; 44)

Next Row K35 (37; 38; 40; 41; 43), K2 tog., K36 (37; 39; 40; 42; 43)

Next Row K35 (36; 38; 39; 41; 42), S1, K1, PSSO, K35 (37; 38; 40; 41; 43)

Next Row K34 (36; 37; 39; 40; 42), K2 tog., K35 (36; 38; 39; 41; 42)

Next Row K34 (35; 37; 38; 40; 41), S1, K1, PSSO, K34 (36; 37; 39; 40; 42)

Next Row K33 (35; 36; 38; 39; 41), K2 tog., K34 (35; 37; 38; 40; 41)

Next Row K33 (34; 36; 37; 39; 40), S1, K1, PSSO, K33 (35; 36; 38; 39; 41)

Next Row K32 (34; 35; 37; 38; 40), K2 tog., K33 (34; 36; 37; 39; 40)

Next Row K32 (33; 35; 36; 38; 39), S1, K1, PSSO, K32 (34; 35; 37; 38; 40)

Next Row K31 (33; 34; 36; 37; 39), K2 tog., K32 (33; 35; 36; 38; 39)

Next Row K31 (32; 34; 35; 37; 38), S1, K1, PSSO, K31 (33; 34; 36; 37; 39)

Next Row K30 (32; 33; 35; 36; 38), K2 tog., K31 (32; 34; 35; 37; 38)

Next Row K30 (31; 33; 34; 36; 37), S1, K1, PSSO, K30 (32; 33; 35; 36; 38)

Next Row K29 (31; 32; 34; 35; 37), K2 tog., K30 (31; 33; 34; 36; 37)

Next Row K29 (30; 32; 33; 35; 36), S1, K1, PSSO, K29 (31; 32; 34; 35; 37)

Next Row K28 (30; 31; 33; 34; 36), K2 tog., K29 (30; 32; 33; 35; 36)

Next Row K28 (29; 31; 32; 34; 35), S1, K1, PSSO, K28 (30; 31; 33; 34; 36)

Next Row K27 (29; 30; 32; 33; 35), K2 tog., K28 (29; 31; 32; 34; 35)

Next Row K27 (28; 30; 31; 33; 34) S1, K1, PSSO, K27 (29; 30; 32; 33; 35)

Next Row K26 (28; 29; 31; 32; 34) K2 tog. K27 (28; 30; 31; 33; 34)

Next Row K26 (27; 29; 30; 32; 33), S1, K1, PSSO, K26 (28; 29; 31; 32; 34)

Next Row K25 (27; 28; 30; 31; 33), K2 tog, K26 (27; 29; 30; 32; 33)

Next Row K25 (26; 28; 29; 31; 32), S1, K1, PSSO, K25 (27; 28; 30; 31; 33)

Next Row K24 (26; 27; 29; 30; 32), K2 tog., K25 (26; 28; 29; 31; 32)

Next Row K24 (25; 27; 28; 30; 31), S1, K1, PSSO, K24 (26; 27; 29; 30; 32)

49 (52; 55; 58; 61; 64) sts. (28 decrease rows) 169 rows.***

Stocking stitch 5 rows.

Next Row K23 (25; 26; 28; 29; 31), K2 tog., K24 (25; 27; 28; 30; 31).

48 (51; 54; 57; 60; 63) sts. 175 rows.

Stocking stitch 17 (17; 14; 11; 8; 5) rows. 192 (192; 189; 186; 183; 180) rows.

Cast off. Remove waste yarn and place first row of main yarn on to holder.

Long length – Hand knit

With waste yarn cast on 83 (86; 89; 92; 95; 98) sts. and work 4 rows in stocking stitch.

With main yarn work 6 rows in stocking stitch.

Next Row K40 (42; 43; 45; 46; 48), K2 tog., K41 (42; 44; 45; 47; 48)

Stocking stitch 5 rows.

Next Row K40 (41; 43; 44; 46; 47), S1, K1, PSSO, K40 (42; 43; 45; 46; 48)

Continue decreasing as follows, working 5 rows in between each decrease row.

Next Row K39 (41; 42; 44; 45; 47), K2 tog., K40 (41; 43; 44; 46; 47)

Next Row K39 (40; 42; 43; 45; 46), S1, K1, PSSO, K39 (41; 42; 44; 45; 47)

Next Row K38 (40; 41; 43; 44; 46), K2 tog., K39 (40; 42; 43; 45; 46)

Next Row K38 (39; 41; 42; 44; 45), S1, K1, PSSO, K38 (40; 41; 43; 44; 46)

Next Row K37 (39; 40; 42; 43; 45), K2 tog., K38 (39; 41; 42; 44; 45)

Next Row K37 (38; 40; 41; 43; 44), S1, K1, PSSO, K37 (39; 40; 42; 43; 45)

Next Row K36 (38; 39; 41; 42; 44), K2 tog., K37 (38; 40; 41; 43; 44)

Next Row K36 (37; 39; 40; 42; 43), S1,K1, PSSO, K36 (38; 39; 41; 42; 44)

Next Row K35 (37; 38; 40; 41; 43), K2 tog., K36 (37; 39; 40; 42; 43)

Next Row K35 (36; 38; 39; 41; 42), S1, K1, PSSO, K35 (37; 38; 40; 41; 43)

Next Row K34 (36; 37; 39; 40; 42), K2 tog., K35 (36; 38; 39; 41; 42)

Next Row K34 (35; 37; 38; 40; 41), S1, K1, PSSO, K34 (36; 37; 39; 40; 42)

Next Row K33 (35; 36; 38; 39; 41), K2 tog., K34 (35; 37; 38; 40; 41)

Next Row K33 (34; 36; 37; 39; 40), S1, K1, PSSO, K33 (35; 36; 38; 39; 41)

Next Row K32 (34; 35; 37; 38; 40), K2 tog., K33 (34; 36; 37; 39; 40)

Next Row K32 (33; 35; 36; 38; 39), S1, K1, PSSO, K32 (34; 35; 37; 38; 40)

Next Row K31 (33; 34; 36; 37; 39), K2 tog., K32 (33; 35; 36; 38; 39)

Next Row K31 (32; 34; 35; 37; 38), S1, K1, PSSO, K31 (33; 34; 36; 37; 39)

Next Row K30 (32; 33; 35; 36; 38), K2 tog., K31 (32; 34; 35; 37; 38)

Next Row K30 (31; 33; 34; 36; 37), S1, K1, PSSO, K30 (32; 33; 35; 36; 38)

Next Row K29 (31; 32; 34; 35; 37), K2 tog., K30 (31; 33; 34; 36; 37)

Next Row K29 (30; 32; 33; 35; 36), S1, K1, PSSO, K29 (31; 32; 34; 35; 37)

Next Row K28 (30; 31; 33; 34; 36), K2 tog., K29 (30; 32; 33; 35; 36)

Next Row K28 (29; 31; 32; 34; 35), S1, K1, PSSO, K28 (30; 31; 33; 34; 36)

Next Row K27 (29; 30; 32; 33; 35), K2 tog., K28 (29; 31; 32; 34; 35)

Next Row K27 (28; 30; 31; 33; 34), S1, K1, PSSO, K27 (29; 30; 32; 33; 35)

Next Row K26 (28; 29; 31; 32; 34), K2 tog., K27 (28; 30; 31; 33; 34)

Next Row K26 (27; 29; 30; 32; 33), S1, K1, PSSO, K26 (28; 29; 31; 32; 34)

Next Row K25 (27; 28; 30; 31; 33), K2 tog., K26 (27; 29; 30; 32; 33)

Next Row K25 (26; 28; 29; 31; 32), S1, K1, PSSO, K25 (27; 28; 30; 31; 33)

Next Row K24 (26; 27; 29; 30; 32), K2 tog., K25 (26; 28; 29; 31; 32)

Next Row K24 (25; 27; 28; 30; 31), S1,K1,PSSO, K24 (26; 27; 29; 30; 32)

49 (52; 55; 58; 61; 64) sts. (34 decrease rows) 205 rows.***

Stocking stitch 5 rows.

Next Row K23 (25; 26; 28; 29; 31), K2 tog., K24 (25; 27; 28; 30; 31)

48 (51; 54; 57; 60; 63) sts. 211 rows.

Stocking stitch 17 (17; 14; 11; 8; 5) rows. 228 (228; 225; 222; 219; 216) rows.

Cast off. Remove waste yarn and place first row of main yarn on to holder.

Flared Side Panel

FOR SLEEVELESS TOP

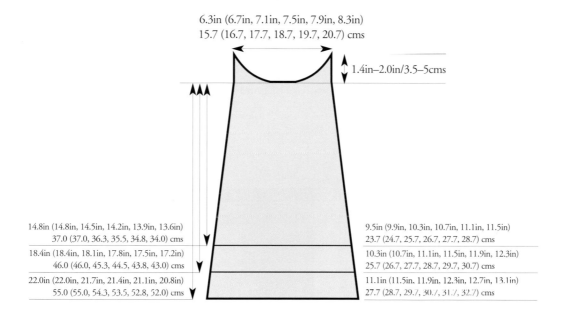

6.3in (6.7in, 7.1in, 7.5in, 7.9in, 8.3in)
15.7 (16.7, 17.7, 18.7, 19.7, 20.7) cms

1.4in–2.0in/3.5–5cms

14.8in (14.8in, 14.5in, 14.2in, 13.9in, 13.6in)
37.0 (37.0, 36.3, 35.5, 34.8, 34.0) cms

18.4in (18.4in, 18.1in, 17.8in, 17.5in, 17.2in)
46.0 (46.0, 45.3, 44.5, 43.8, 43.0) cms

22.0in (22.0in, 21.7in, 21.4in, 21.1in, 20.8in)
55.0 (55.0, 54.3, 53.5, 52.8, 52.0) cms

9.5in (9.9in, 10.3in, 10.7in, 11.1in, 11.5in)
23.7 (24.7, 25.7, 26.7, 27.7, 28.7) cms

10.3in (10.7in, 11.1in, 11.5in, 11.9in, 12.3in)
25.7 (26.7, 27.7, 28.7, 29.7, 30.7) cms

11.1in (11.5in, 11.9in, 12.3in, 12.7in, 13.1in)
27.7 (28.7, 29.7, 30.7, 31.7, 32.7) cms

Hand or Machine knit

Work as for flared side panel for top with sleeves to *** . 49 (52; 55; 58; 61; 64) sts.
133 rows for short length, 169 rows for medium length, 205 rows for long length.
Work 15 (15; 12; 9; 6; 3) rows in stocking stitch.
148 (148; 145; 142; 139; 136) rows for short length, 184 (184; 181; 178; 175;
172) rows for medium length,
220 (220; 217; 214; 211; 208) rows for long length.

Shape armhole

Work 14 (15; 16; 17; 18; 19) sts. and leave remaining 35 (37; 39; 41; 43; 45) sts.
on hold position for machine knitting or turn for hand knitting.

Next Row Work 2 tog., work 12 (13; 14; 15; 16; 17) sts.

Next Row Work 11 (12; 13; 14; 15; 16) sts. Work 2 tog.

Continue decreasing on every row until 1 stitch remains, cast off.

Rejoin yarn to remaining stitches, cast off 21 (22; 23; 24; 25; 26) sts. and
work to end.

Next Row Work 12 (13; 14; 15; 16; 17) sts. Work 2 tog.

Next Row Work 2 tog., work 11 (12; 13; 14; 15; 16) sts.

Continue decreasing on every row until 1 stitch remains, cast off.

162 (163; 161; 159; 157; 155) rows for short length, 198 (199; 197; 195; 193; 191)
rows for medium length and 234 (235; 233; 231; 229; 227) rows for long length.

Remove waste yarn and place first row of main yarn on to holder.

Flared side panel for sleeveless top.

Waistcoat with flared side panels.

Facing page: Waistcoat: flared side panels; short length.

Sleeves for Square Armhole

LONG/SHORT

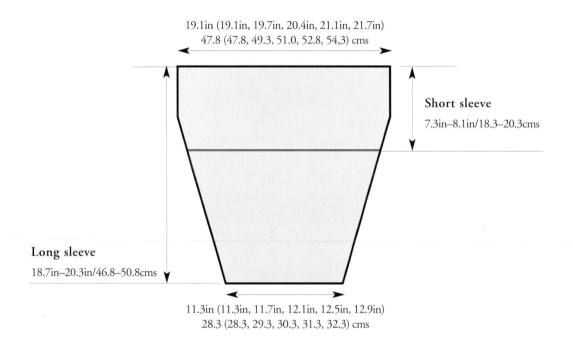

19.1in (19.1in, 19.7in, 20.4in, 21.1in, 21.7in)
47.8 (47.8, 49.3, 51.0, 52.8, 54,3) cms

Short sleeve

7.3in–8.1in/18.3–20.3cms

Long sleeve

18.7in–20.3in/46.8–50.8cms

11.3in (11.3in, 11.7in, 12.1in, 12.5in, 12.9in)
28.3 (28.3, 29.3, 30.3, 31.3, 32.3) cms

(For side panels see p. 28)

Long sleeves

The sleeves are worked from the top downwards. Work same size as side panel.

Method of decreasing

Hand Knit   K1, K2 tog., knit to last 3 sts., S1, K1, PSSO, K1.

Machine Knit Using 2-hole transfer hook take end two stitches on right side of work and move one stitch to left so that decrease is worked on 2nd stitch from the edge, then move the end two stitches on left side of work one stitch to the right.

With waste yarn and beginning with knit row (hand) or carriage on left (machine), cast on 143 (143; 148; 153; 158; 163) sts. and work 4 rows in stocking stitch.

With main yarn work 33 (33; 35; 37; 39; 41) rows in stocking stitch.

Place marker here for beginning of sleeve seam and centre of side panel.

Work 5 rows in stocking stitch.

(Adjust here for length of sleeve or see note 3 on p. 7)

First and Second Size

Decrease 1 stitch at each end of next then every following 4th row 12 times, (13 in all) (117sts.).

Decrease 1 stitch at each end of every following 6th row 16 times (85sts.).

Third Size

Decrease 1 stitch at each end of next then every following 4th row 14 times, (15 in all) (118sts.).

Decrease 1 stitch at each end of every following 6th row 15 times (88sts.).

Fourth Size

Decrease 1 stitch at each end of next then every following 4th row 16 times (17 in all) (119sts.).

Decrease 1 stitch at each end of every following 6th row 14 times (91sts.).

Fifth Size

Decrease 1 stitch at each end of next then every following 4th row 18 times (19 in all) (120sts.).

Decrease 1 stitch at each end of every following 6th row 13 times (94sts.).

Sixth Size

Decrease 1 stitch at each end of next then every following 4th row 20 times (21 in all). (121sts.)

Decrease 1 stitch at each end of every following 6th row 12 times, (97sts.).

All Sizes

Work 4 rows in stocking stitch. 187 (187; 191; 195; 199; 203) rows.

If machine knitting place stitches on needle and continue with cuff.

Fitted cuff *(Hand knit)*

Wrong Side Work 1 row decreasing as follows:

1st and 2nd Sizes: P3, *P2 tog., P5, Rep. from * to last 5sts., P2 tog. P3.

3rd Size: P1, *P2 tog., P4, Rep. from * to last 3 sts., P2 tog., P1.

4th Size: P2 ,*P2 tog., P3, Rep. from * to last 4 sts., P2 tog., P2.

5th Size: P2 ,*P2 tog., P4, P2 tog., P3, Rep. from * to last 4 sts., P2 tog. P2.

6th Size: P4, *P2 tog., P3, P2 tog., P2, Rep. from * to last 3 sts., P3.

73 (73; 73; 73; 77; 77) sts.

MOCK CABLE PATTERN

Row 1 P1, *K3, P1, Rep. from * to end.

Row 2 K1, *P3, K1, Rep. from * to end.

Row 3 P1, *S1, K2, PSSO and *at the same time knit into slip stitch*, P1.
        Rep. from * to end.

Row 4 As Row 2.

With right side facing, work cable pattern beginning with Row 3, until
6 cable rows have been completed. Work Rows 4, 1 and 2 again. 24 rows.

Sizes 1; 2; 3; & 4.

Next Row Decrease 1 stitch in every other cable as follows:

*P1, S1, K2, PSSO and knit; P1, S1, K2, PSSO; Rep. from * to last stitch, P1.

Sizes 5 & 6

Next Row Decrease 1 stitch in every other cable as follows:

*P1, S1, K2, PSSO and knit; P1, S1, K2, PSSO; Rep. from * to last 5 sts.,

P1, S1, K2, PSSO and knit, P1.

Work 1 row in pattern as set. Cast off in pattern.

Remove waste yarn from
top of sleeve and cast off
loosely.

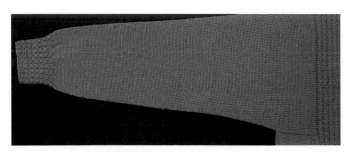

Long sleeve for square armhole

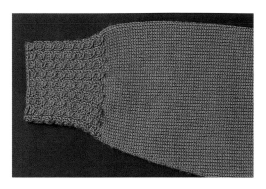

Fitted cuff.

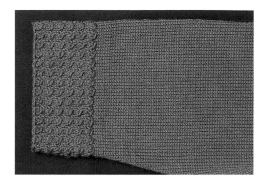

Loose cuff.

Loose cuff *(Hand knit)*

Wrong Side Work 1 row increasing as follows: K1, *P2, inc. in next st. by purling into front and knitting into back. Rep. from * to end.

With right side facing, work cable pattern (see fitted cuff) beginning with Row 3, until 5 cable rows have been completed. Work Rows 4, 1 and 2 again. 20 rows.

Next Row Decrease 1 stitch in every cable as follows: P1, *S1, K2, PSSO, P1, Rep. from * to end.

Next Row (K1, P2) to last stitch, K1.

Cast off in pattern. Remove waste yarn from top of sleeve and cast off loosely.

Short sleeves

The sleeves are worked from the top downwards. Work sleeve the same size as side panel.

Method of decreasing

Hand Knit K1, K2 tog. knit to last 3 sts., S1, K1, PSSO, K1.

Machine Knit Using 2-hole transfer hook take end 2 stitches on right side of work and move 1 stitch to left so that decrease is worked on 2nd stitch from the edge, then move the end 2 stitches on left side of work 1 stitch to the right.

With waste yarn and beginning with knit row (hand) or carriage on left (machine), cast on 144 (144; 147; 153; 159; 162) sts. and work 4 rows in stocking stitch.

With main yarn work 33 (33; 35; 37; 39; 41) rows in stocking stitch.

Place marker here for beginning of sleeve seam and centre of side panel.

Work 1 row. (Adjust here for length of sleeve.)

Decrease 1 stitch at each end of next and every following 4th row until 124 (124; 127; 133; 139; 142) sts.

Work 2 rows. 73 (73; 75; 77; 79; 81) rows.

If machine knitting place stitches on needle and continue with cuff.

Loose cuff *(Hand knit)*

Wrong Side Work 1 row increasing as follows: K1, *P2, inc. in next st. by purling into front and knitting into back. Rep. from * to end.

With right side facing, work cable pattern (see fitted cuff, long sleeve, on p. 44) beginning with Row 3, until 3 cable rows have been completed. Work Rows 4, 1 and 2 again. 12 rows.

Next Row Decrease 1 stitch in every cable as follows: P1, *S1, K2, PSSO, P1. Rep. from * to end.

Next Row (K1, P2) to last stitch, K1.

Cast off in pattern. Remove waste yarn from top of sleeve and cast off loosely.

Fitted cuff *(Hand knit)*

Wrong Side Purl 1 row increasing as follows:

1st and 2nd Size: Increase 1 stitch at beg. of row.

3rd Size: Increase 1 stitch at each end of row.

4th Size: No Increase.

5th Size: Increase 1 stitch at each end of row.

6th Size: Increase 1 stitch at each end and 1 stitch in the middle of row (71st stitch).

125 (125; 129; 133; 141; 145) sts.

Continue as for loose cuff from #.

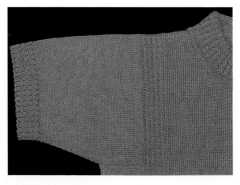

Short sleeve.

Cape Sleeves

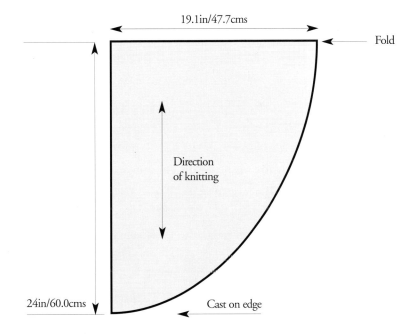

19.1in/47.7cms

Fold

Direction
of knitting

24in/60.0cms

Cast on edge

Machine knit – work 2

See diagram for direction of knitting.   Place markers, where indicated, on curved edge.

Place work at left-hand side of needle bed to allow for increasing at right-hand edge. With carriage on right, cast on 4 sts. and work 1 row to left.

Next Row Inc. 1 st. on right-hand side (fully fashioned) as follows:

Transfer end stitch on to next empty needle so that 2nd needle from end becomes empty, and pick up loop of 2nd stitch from previous row and place on needle that has become empty.

Next Row Inc. 3 sts. on right-hand side (e wrap). Rep. last 2 rows 5 times. (28sts. 13 rows). Place marker.

Next Row Inc. 1 stitch on right-hand side (fully fashioned).

Next Row Inc. 2 sts. on right-hand side (e wrap). (31 sts. 15 rows)

Rep. last 2 rows 7 times. (52 sts. 29 rows) Place marker.

Next Row Inc. 1 stitch on right-hand side every row for 26 rows. (Increase by bringing forward next needle into working position.) (78 sts. 55 rows)

Place marker.

Work 1 row.

Increase 1 stitch on right-hand side on next 2 rows.

Rep. last 3 rows 13 more times. (106 sts. 97 rows) Place marker.

Work 1 row.

Increase 1 stitch on right-hand side on next row then every other row 16 more times. (123 sts. 131 rows) Place marker.

Work 2 rows.

Increase 1 stitch on right-hand side on next row then every following 3rd row 5 more times. (129 sts. 149 rows) Place marker.

Work 3 rows.

Increase 1 stitch on right-hand side on next row then every following 4th row 4 more times. (134 sts. 169 rows) Place marker.

Work 4 rows.

Increase 1 stitch on right-hand side on next row then every following 5th row 3 more times. (138 sts. 189 rows) Place marker.

Work 5 rows.

Increase 1 stitch on right-hand side on next row then every following 6th row 2 more times. (141 sts. 207 rows) Place marker.

Work 6 rows.

Increase 1 stitch on right-hand side on next row then following 7th row. (143 sts. 221 rows) Place marker.

Work 18 rows without shaping and place marker each end of last row for centre of cape sleeve and top of shoulder. 239 rows.

Re-set row counter to 000. Work a further 19 rows without shaping. Place marker.

Pictured opposite: Cape suit; long length; flared side panels; cape sleeves; straight skirt.

Keeping the decreasing on the same side as the increasing continue as follows:

Decrease 1 stitch on next row. Work 6 rows.

Rep. last 7 rows once. (141sts. 33 rows) Place marker.

Decrease 1 stitch on next row. Work 5 rows.

Rep. last 6 rows twice. (138sts. 51 rows) Place marker.

Decrease 1 stitch on next row. Work 4 rows.

Rep. last 5 rows 3 times. (134sts. 71 rows) Place marker.

Decrease 1 stitch on next row. Work 3 rows.

Rep. last 4 rows 4 times. (129sts. 91 rows) Place marker.

Decrease 1 stitch on next row. Work 2 rows.

Rep. last 3 rows 5 times. (123sts. 109 rows) Place marker.

Decrease 1 stitch on next row. Work 1 row.

Rep. last 2 rows 16 times. (106sts. 143 rows) Place marker.

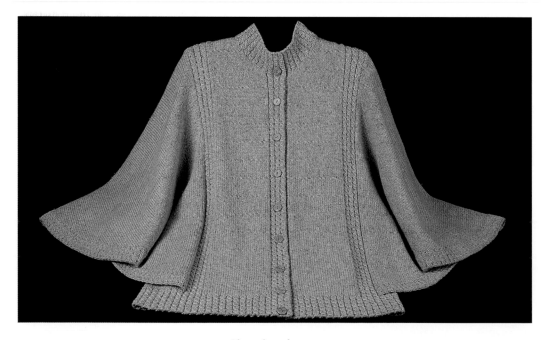

Short length cape.

Decrease 1 stitch on next 2 rows. Work 1 row.
Rep. last 3 rows 13 times. (78sts. 185 rows) Place marker.

Decrease 1 stitch on every row for 26 rows. (52sts. 211 rows) Place marker.

Cast off 2 sts. on next row. Decrease 1 st. on next row.
Rep. last 2 rows 7 times. (28 sts. 227 rows) Place marker.

Cast off 3 sts. on next row. Decrease 1 st. on next row.
Rep. last 2 rows 5 times. (4 sts. 239 rows). Cast off.

Hand knit – work 2

See diagram for direction of knitting. Place markers, where indicated, on curved edge.

Method of increasing

Increase in knit row by casting on stitch/es at beginning of row. (Insert right-hand needle in between first 2 stitches on left-hand needle, pull yarn through and place on left-hand needle.)
Increase in purl row by purling twice into the last stitch (first into the front and then into the back of the stitch).

Method of decreasing

K2tog. at beginning of row and P2tog. at end of row.

Cast on 4sts. and knit 1 row.
Next Row Purl, increase in last stitch.
Next Row Cast on 3sts., knit to end.
Rep. last 2 rows 5 times. (28sts., 13 rows) Place marker.

Next Row Purl, increase in last stitch.
Next Row Cast on 2 sts., knit to end.
Rep. last 2 rows 7 times. (52sts., 29 rows) Place marker.

Next Row Purl, increase in last stitch.

Next Row Cast on 1 stitch, knit to end.

Rep. last 2 rows until 78 sts. (55 rows) Place marker.

Keeping continuity of stocking stitch work 1 row.

Increase 1 stitch on sleeve edge (curve) of work on next 2 rows.

Rep. last 3 rows 13 more times. (106 sts. 97 rows) Place marker.

Work 1 row.

Increase 1 stitch on sleeve edge (curve) of work on next row then every other row 16 more times. (123 sts., 131 rows) Place marker.

Work 2 rows.

Increase 1 stitch on sleeve edge (curve) of work on next row then every following 3rd row 5 more times. (129 sts., 149 rows) Place marker.

Work 3 rows.

Increase 1 stitch on sleeve edge (curve) of work on next row then every following 4th row 4 more times. (134 sts., 169 rows) Place marker.

Work 4 rows.

Increase 1 stitch on sleeve edge (curve) of work on next row then every following 5th row 3 more times. (138 sts., 189 rows) Place marker.

Work 5 rows.

Increase 1 stitch on sleeve edge (curve) of work on next row then every following 6th row 2 more times. (141 sts., 207 rows) Place marker.

Work 6 rows.

Increase 1 stitch on sleeve edge (curve) of work on next row then following 7th row. (143 sts., 221 rows) Place marker.

Work 18 rows without shaping and place marker each end of last row for centre of cape sleeve and top of shoulder. (239 rows)

Re-start row count. Work a further 19 rows without shaping. Place marker.

Keeping the decreasing on the same side as the increasing continue as follows:

Decrease 1 stitch on next row. Work 6 rows.

Rep. last 7 rows once. (141 sts., 33 rows) Place marker.

Decrease 1 stitch on next row. Work 5 rows.

Rep. last 6 rows twice. (138 sts., 51 rows) Place marker.

Decrease 1 stitch on next row. Work 4 rows.

Rep. last 5 rows 3 times. (134 sts., 71 rows) Place marker.

Decrease 1 stitch on next row. Work 3 rows.

Rep. last 4 rows 4 times. (129 sts., 91 rows) Place marker.

Decrease 1 stitch on next row. Work 2 rows.

Rep. last 3 rows 5 times. (123 sts., 109 rows) Place marker.

Decrease 1 stitch on next row. Work 1 row.

Rep. last 2 rows 16 times. (106 sts., 143 rows) Place marker.

Decrease 1 stitch on next 2 rows. Work 1 row.

Rep. last 3 rows 13 times.   (78 sts., 185 rows) Place marker.

Decrease 1 stitch on every row for 26 rows. (52 sts., 211 rows) Place marker.

Cast off 2 sts. on next row. Decrease 1 st. on next row.

Rep. last 2 rows 7 times. (28 sts., 227 rows) Place marker.

Cast off 3 sts. on next row. Decrease 1 st. on next row.

Rep. last 2 rows 5 times. (4 sts., 239 rows) Cast off.

Side panels with shaped armhole

FOR TOP WITH SLEEVES

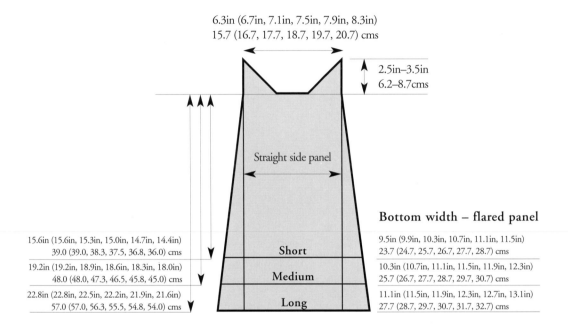

6.3in (6.7in, 7.1in, 7.5in, 7.9in, 8.3in)
15.7 (16.7, 17.7, 18.7, 19.7, 20.7) cms

2.5in–3.5in
6.2–8.7cms

Straight side panel

Bottom width – flared panel

15.6in (15.6in, 15.3in, 15.0in, 14.7in, 14.4in)
39.0 (39.0, 38.3, 37.5, 36.8, 36.0) cms

19.2in (19.2in, 18.9in, 18.6in, 18.3in, 18.0in)
48.0 (48.0, 47.3, 46.5, 45.8, 45.0) cms

22.8in (22.8in, 22.5in, 22.2in, 21.9in, 21.6in)
57.0 (57.0, 56.3, 55.5, 54.8, 54.0) cms

9.5in (9.9in, 10.3in, 10.7in, 11.1in, 11.5in)
23.7 (24.7, 25.7, 26.7, 27.7, 28.7) cms

10.3in (10.7in, 11.1in, 11.5in, 11.9in, 12.3in)
25.7 (26.7, 27.7, 28.7, 29.7, 30.7) cms

11.1in (11.5in, 11.9in, 12.3in, 12.7in, 13.1in)
27.7 (28.7, 29.7, 30.7, 31.7, 32.7) cms

Short

Medium

Long

Work as for side panel for top with sleeves, pages 28–38 (either straight or flared)
but do not cast off.

Ending with:

47 (50; 53; 56; 59; 62) sts. straight side panel.

48 (51; 54; 57; 60; 63) sts. flared side panel.

156 (156; 153; 150; 147; 144) rows short length.

192 (192; 189; 186; 183; 180) rows medium length.

228 (228; 225; 222; 219; 216) rows long length.

NOTE

Hand Knit   Work 4 rows extra on 1st Size and 1 row extra on 3rd and 5th Sizes. The last row before shaping the armhole should be a purl row.

Machine Knit Work 3 rows extra on 1st Size only.

Method of decreasing

Machine Knit Take off 2 edge stitches using 2-hole transfer hook then next stitch using 1-hole transfer hook. Move stitches on 2-hole transfer hook across then replace stitch on 1-hole transfer hook on to end but one needle.

Hand Knit At beg. of row: K1, S1, K1, PSSO.

At end of row: Knit to last 3 sts., K2 tog., K1.

Round-neck coat: flared side panels; long sleeves.

Shape armhole

Work 15 (16; 17; 18; 19; 20) sts. and leave remaining stitches on hold position for machine knitting or holder for hand knitting.

*Work 1 row.

Decrease 1 stitch on centre side (armhole) on next and every other row until 2 sts. remain. Cast off. **

Rejoin yarn to remaining stitches.

Cast off 17 (18; 19; 20; 21; 22) sts. for straight side panel and work to end. (Underarm stitches)

Cast off 18 (19; 20; 21; 22; 23) sts. for flared side panel and work to end. (Underarm stitches)

Repeat from * to **.

Remove waste yarn and place first row of main yarn on to holder.

Front view of shaped armhole.

Underarm view of shaped armhole.

Sleeves for Shaped Armhole

LONG, SHORT & THREE-QUARTER

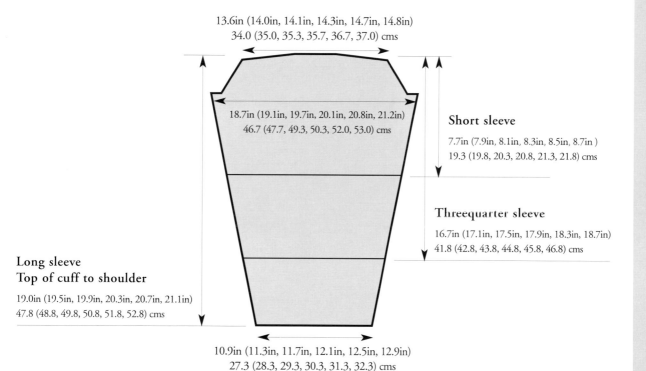

13.6in (14.0in, 14.1in, 14.3in, 14.7in, 14.8in)
34.0 (35.0, 35.3, 35.7, 36.7, 37.0) cms

18.7in (19.1in, 19.7in, 20.1in, 20.8in, 21.2in)
46.7 (47.7, 49.3, 50.3, 52.0, 53.0) cms

Short sleeve

7.7in (7.9in, 8.1in, 8.3in, 8.5in, 8.7in)
19.3 (19.8, 20.3, 20.8, 21.3, 21.8) cms

Threequarter sleeve

16.7in (17.1in, 17.5in, 17.9in, 18.3in, 18.7in)
41.8 (42.8, 43.8, 44.8, 45.8, 46.8) cms

Long sleeve
Top of cuff to shoulder

19.0in (19.5in, 19.9in, 20.3in, 20.7in, 21.1in)
47.8 (48.8, 49.8, 50.8, 51.8, 52.8) cms

10.9in (11.3in, 11.7in, 12.1in, 12.5in, 12.9in)
27.3 (28.3, 29.3, 30.3, 31.3, 32.3) cms

Method of increasing

Machine Knit Transfer end stitch on left-hand side, one needle to left, and take loop under second stitch from left side on to empty needle. Transfer end stitch on right-hand side, one needle to right, and take loop under second stitch from right on to empty needle and work across all stitches.

Hand Knit Pick up loop in between first and second stitch from each edge, knit into the back of it on knit row and purl into back of it on purl row.

Method of decreasing

Machine Knit Take off 2 edge stitches using 2-hole transfer hook then next stitch using 1-hole transfer hook. Move stitches on 2-hole transfer hook across then replace stitch on 1-hole transfer hook on to end but one needle.

Hand Knit At beg. of knit row: K1, S1, K1, PSSO.

At end of knit row: Knit to last 3 sts., K2 tog., K1.

At beg. of purl row: P1, P2 tog.

At end of purl row: Purl to last 3 sts., P2 tog., tbl. P1.

NOTE To add more rows to the length, increase the number of increasings every 6th row and decrease (by the same amount) the number of increasings every 4th row. This will give you an extra 2 rows each time. To shorten the length, work in reverse.

Long sleeve

With waste yarn and beginning with knit row (hand) or carriage on left (machine), cast on 82 (85; 88; 91; 94; 97) sts. and work 4 rows in stocking stitch.

With main yarn work 4 rows in stocking stitch.

First Size

Increase 1 stitch each end of next and every following 6th row 16 times, 116 sts.

Increase 1 stitch each end of every following 4th row 12 times, 140 sts. (149 rows)

Second Size

Increase 1 stitch each end of next and every following 6th row 17 times, 121 sts.

Increase 1 stitch each end of every following 4th row 11 times, 143 sts. (151 rows)

Third Size

Increase 1 stitch each end of next and every following 6th row 16 times, 122 sts.

Increase 1 stitch each end of every following 4th row 13 times, 148 sts. (153 rows)

Fourth Size

Increase 1 stitch each end of next and every following 6th row 17 times, 127 sts.

Increase 1 stitch each end of every following 4th row 12 times, 151 sts. (155 rows)

Fifth Size

Increase 1 stitch each end of next and every following 6th row 16 times, 128 sts.

Increase 1 stitch each end of every following 4th row 14 times, 156 sts (157 rows)

Sixth Size

Increase 1 stitch each end of next and every following 6th row 17 times, 133 sts.

Increase 1 stitch each end of every following 4th row 13 times, 159 sts. (159 rows)

All Sizes

Work 9 rows without shaping. 158 (160; 162; 164; 166; 168) rows.

(Hand knitting ends with purl row.) Place marker each end.

Shape top of sleeve

Cast off 10 (10; 11; 11; 12; 12) sts. at beg. of next 2 rows.

120 (123; 126; 129; 132; 135) sts. Work 1 row.

Decrease 1 stitch at each end of next and every 3rd row until 102 (105; 106; 107; 110; 111) sts. 9 (9; 10; 11; 11; 12) decreasings.

Work 1 (3; 2; 1; 3; 2) row(s). 187 (191; 195; 199; 203; 207) rows.

Machine Knit

Leave length of yarn long enough to cast off all stitches at end.

All Sizes

Next Row Leave 10 sts. at each end on hold and work across remaining centre stitches.

1st Size

Rep. 3 times. Cast off 102 sts.

2nd, 3rd & 4th Sizes

Rep. twice.

Next Row Leave 11 sts. at each end on hold and work across remaining stitches.

Cast off 105 (106; 107) sts.

5th & 6th Sizes

Rep. once.

Next Row Leave 11 sts. at each end on hold and work across remaining stitches.

Rep. once. Cast off 110 (111) sts.

191 (195; 199; 203; 207; 211) rows.

Remove waste yarn from cast-on edge of sleeve and place stitches on needle to knit cuff.

Hand Knit

Leave length of yarn long enough to cast off all stitches at end.

Sizes 1; 2; 5; & 6.

Next Row Slip 10 sts. purlwise, join in new yarn and knit to last 10 sts., turn.

Next Row Break off yarn and slip 10 sts., join in new yarn and purl to last 20 sts. turn,

Next Row Break off yarn, slip 10 (10; 11; 11) sts. purlwise, join in new yarn and knit to last 30 (30; 31; 31) sts., turn.

Next Row Break off yarn, slip 10 (11; 11; 11) sts., join in new yarn and purl to last 40 (41; 42; 42) sts., break off yarn.

Sizes 3 & 4.

Next Row Slip 10 sts. purlwise, join in new yarn and purl to last 10 sts., turn,

Next Row Break off yarn and slip 10 sts., join in new yarn and knit to last 20 sts., turn.

Next Row Break off yarn, slip 10 sts. purlwise, join in new yarn and purl to last 30 sts., turn.

Next Row Break off yarn, slip 11 sts., join in new yarn and knit to last 41 sts., break off yarn.

Next Row With original yarn cast off across row, 102 (105; 106; 107; 110; 111) sts., 191 (195; 199; 203; 207; 211) rows.

Remove waste yarn from cast-on edge of sleeve and place stitches on needle to knit cuff.

Fitted cuff (Hand knit)

Wrong Side Work 1 row decreasing as follows:

1st Size P4, *P2 tog., P7, Rep. from * to last 6 sts., P2 tog. P4.

2nd Size P3, *P2 tog., P5, Rep. from * to last 5 sts., P2 tog. P3.

3rd Size P1, *P2 tog., P4, Rep. from * to last 3 sts,. P2 tog. P1.

4th Size P2 ,*P2 tog., P3, Rep. from * to last 4 sts., P2 tog. P2.

5th Size P2 ,*P2 tog., P4, P2 tog., P3, Rep. from * to last 4 sts., P2 tog., P2.

6th Size P4, *P2 tog., P3, P2 tog., P2, Rep. from * to last 3 sts., P3.

73 (73; 73; 73; 77; 77) sts.

MOCK CABLE PATTERN

Row 1 P1, *K3, P1, Rep. from * to end.

Row 2 K1, *P3, K1, Rep. from * to end.

Row 3 P1, *S1, K2, PSSO and *at the same time knit into slip stitch*, P1,
Rep. from * to end.

Row 4 As row 2.

With right side facing, work cable pattern beginning with Row 3, until 6 cable rows have been completed. Work Rows 4, 1 and 2 again. (24 rows)

Sizes 1; 2; 3; & 4.

Next Row Decrease 1 stitch in every other cable as follows:

*P1, S1, K2, PSSO and knit; P1, S1, K2, PSSO;

Rep. from * to last stitch, P1.

Sizes 5 & 6

Next Row Decrease 1 stitch in every other cable as follows: *P1, S1, K2, PSSO and knit; P1, S1, K2, PSSO; Rep. from * to last 5 sts., P1, S1, K2, PSSO and knit, P1. Work 1 row in pattern as set. Cast off in pattern.

Loose cuff (Hand knit)

Wrong Side Work 1 row increasing as follows:

K1, *P2, inc. in next st. by purling into front and knitting into back.

Rep. from * to end.

With right side facing, work cable pattern (see fitted cuff) beginning with Row 3, until 5 cable rows have been completed. Work Rows 4, 1 and 2 again. (20 rows)

Next Row Dec.1 stitch in every cable as follows: P1, *S1, K2, PSSO, P1.

Rep. from * to end.

Next Row (K1, P2) to last stitch, K1. Cast off in pattern.

Short sleeve

NOTE If you would prefer a narrower armhole and sleeve for a summer top then deduct 6 sts. from the width of the sleeve and work 4 rows less on the back and front (after armhole shaping and before neck shaping).

With waste yarn and beginning with knit row (hand) or carriage on left (machine), cast on 120 (125; 130; 133; 138; 143) sts. and work 4 rows in stocking stitch.

With main yarn continue in stocking stitch and work 3 (5; 5; 5; 5; 4) rows.

Increase each end of next and every following 4th (4th; 4th; 4th; 4th; 5th) row until 140 (143; 148; 151; 156; 159) sts.

Work 4 (6; 6; 6; 6; 4) rows without shaping. (44 rows)

(Adjust for length, if necessary) Place marker.

Shape top of sleeve

Work as for long sleeve. 77 (79; 81; 83; 85; 87) rows.

Remove waste yarn from cast-on edge of sleeve and place stitches on needle to knit cuff.

Fitted cuff (*Hand knit*)

With right side facing knit 1 row increasing or decreasing evenly where necessary to 121 (125; 129; 133; 141; 145) sts.

Beginning with Row 2, work cable pattern (see long sleeve) until 4 cable rows have been completed.

Work Rows 4, 1 and 2 again. (16 rows)

Next Row Dec. 1 stitch in every cable as follows: P1, *S1, K2, PSSO, P1.
Rep. from * to end.
Next Row (K1, P2) to last stitch, K1. Cast off in pattern.

Loose cuff (*Hand knit*)
Work as for Fitted Cuff but increase evenly to 157 (165; 173; 177; 185; 189) sts.

Three-quarter sleeve
With waste yarn cast on 90 (93; 96; 99; 102; 105) sts. and work 4 rows in stocking stitch.
With main yarn continue in stocking stitch and work 4 rows. Hand knit start with knit row.
Inc. 1 stitch each end of next and every foll. 6th row 12 (13; 12; 13; 12; 13) times.
116 (121; 122; 127; 128; 133) sts., 77 (83; 77; 83; 77; 83) rows.
Inc. 1 stitch each end of every foll. 4th row 12 (11; 13; 12; 14; 13) times.
140 (143; 148; 151; 156; 159) sts., 125 (127; 129; 131; 133; 135) rows.
Work 9 rows without shaping. 134 (136; 138; 140; 142; 144) rows. Place marker.

Shape top of sleeve
Work as for Long Sleeve 167 (171; 175; 179; 183; 187) rows.
Remove waste yarn from cast on edge of sleeve and place stitches on needle
to knit cuff.

Fitted cuff (Hand knit)
With right side facing, decrease evenly to 89 (89; 93; 97; 97; 101) sts. and work as for
Short Sleeve beginning with Row 2.

Loose cuff (Hand knit)
With right side facing, knit 1 row increasing 1 stitch in centre.
Continue as for Long Sleeve starting with wrong side increase row, but work one less
cable before decrease row.

Mock Cable Bands

HAND KNIT

Side bands for tops with sleeves

Work 2 (Size 3mm needles)

These are knitted from the top downwards and joined together at the top.

CABLE PATTERN

Row 1 P1, (P1, K3) 4 times, P2.

Row 2 K1, (K1, P3) 4 times, K2.

Row 3 P1, (P1, S1, K2, PSSO and *at the same time knit into slip stitch*) 4 times, P2.

Row 4 As Row 2.

NOTE First figure for short length, figures in brackets for medium and long lengths respectively.

With waste yarn cast on 19sts. and work 5 rows in stocking stitch.

Change to main yarn and work Row 4 of cable pattern.

Work the 4 rows of cable pattern, starting with Row 1, 63 (72; 81) times, 253 (289; 325) rows.

Leave stitches on holder for bottom band.

Remove waste yarn and carefully place 19sts. of first row of main yarn on to needle.

With right side facing, rejoin main yarn and starting with Row 1 continue in pattern until 63 (72; 81) cables are completed, 252 (288; 324) rows.

Leave sts. on holder for bottom band.

Side bands for tops without sleeves

(Size 3 mm needles)

These are knitted from the top downwards and joined together at the top.

Right side band – front

CABLE PATTERN

Row 1 P1, (K3, P1) 4 times, P1.

Row 2 K2, (P3, K1) 4 times.

Row 3 P1, (S1, K2, PSSO and *at the same time knit into slip stitch*, P1) 4 times, P1.

Row 4 As Row 2.

With waste yarn cast on 18sts. and work 5 rows in stocking stitch.

Change to main yarn and work 76 (76; 78; 80; 82; 84) rows in pattern starting with Row 4.

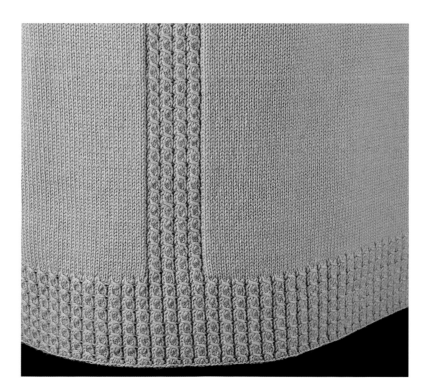

Mock cable bands, showing side and bottom details.

Next Row Work in pattern and increase in last stitch. 19sts.

Continue in cable pattern, as band for top with sleeves, to required length and leave stitches on holder for bottom band.

253 rows for short length, 289 rows for medium length and 325 rows for long length. Remove waste yarn and carefully place 18sts. of first row of main yarn on to needle. Continue with right side band – back.

Right side band – back

With right side facing and using main yarn, start with Row 1 and work in pattern as follows:

Row 1 P2, (K3, P1) 4 times.

Row 2 K1, (P3, K1) 4 times, K1.

Row 3 P2, (S1, K2, PSSO and *at the same time knit into slip stitch*, P1) 4 times.

Row 4 As Row 2.

Continue in pattern until 75 (75; 77; 79; 81; 83) rows have been completed.

Next Row Increase in first stitch, pattern to end. 19sts.

Continue in cable pattern, as band for top with sleeves, to required length and leave stitches on holder for bottom band.

252 rows for short length, 288 rows for medium length and 324 rows for long length.

Left side band – front

CABLE PATTERN

Row 1 P2, (K3, P1) 4 times.

Row 2 K1, (P3, K1) 4 times, K1.

Row 3 P2, (S1, K2, PSSO and *at the same time knit into slip stitch, P1)* 4 times.

Row 4 As Row 2.

With waste yarn cast on 18 sts. and work 5 rows in stocking stitch.

Change to main yarn and work 76 (76; 78; 80; 82; 84) rows in pattern starting with Row 4.

Next Row Increase in first stitch, pattern to end. 19 sts.

Continue in cable pattern, as band for top with sleeves, to required length and leave stitches on holder for bottom band.

253 rows for short length, 289 rows for medium length and 325 rows for long length.

Remove waste yarn and carefully place 18 sts. of first row of main yarn on to needle. Continue with left side band – back.

Left side band – back

With right side facing and using main yarn, start with Row 1 and work in pattern as follows:

Row 1 P1, (K3, P1) 4 times, P1.

Row 2 K2, (P3, K1) 4 times.

Row 3 P1, (S1, K2, PSSO and *at the same time knit into slip stitch*, P1) 4 times, P1.

Row 4 As Row 2.

Continue in cable pattern until 75 (75; 77; 79; 81; 83) rows have been completed.

Next Row Work in pattern and increase in last stitch. 19 sts.

Continue in pattern, as band for top with sleeves, to required length and leave stitches on holder for bottom band.

252 rows for short length, 288 rows for medium length and 324 rows for long length.

Neckbands for round-neck Jumper, Tunic or Dress
(See also Alternative Neckbands)

CABLE PATTERN

Row 1 P1, *K3, P1, Rep. from * to end.

Row 2 K1, *P3, K1, Rep. from * to end.

Row 3 P1, *S1, K2, PSSO *and at the same time knit into slip stitch*, P1.
　　　　Rep. from * to end.

Row 4 As Row 2.

Graft together right shoulder seam.

With size 2.75 mm. needles, pick up stitches around neck as follows:
With right side facing, pick up 13 (14; 14; 15; 15; 16) sts. down straight of left front neck, 23 sts. down curve, 19 (21; 21; 23; 23; 25) sts. across front (cast-off sts.) 23 sts. up curve of right front neck, and 13 (14; 14; 15; 15; 16) sts. up straight of right front neck, 4 sts. down curve of right back neck, 43 (45; 45; 47; 47; 50) sts. across back (cast-off sts.) and 4 sts. up curve of left back neck 42 (148; 148; 154; 154; 161) sts.

Next Row

1st Size	P5, inc. in next st. (P4, inc. in next st.) 26 times, P6. 169 sts.
2nd & 3rd Sizes	P3, inc. in next st. (P4, inc. in next st.) 28 times, P4. 177 sts.
4th & 5th Sizes	P1, inc. in next st. (P4, inc. in next st.) 30 times, P2. 185 sts.
6th Size	P2, inc. in next st. (P4, inc. in next st.) 31 times, P3. 193 sts.

Single-thickness neckband

Starting with Row 3 of cable pattern, work until 4 cable rows have been completed. Change to size 2.25 mm needles and work a further 3 rows.

Next Cable Row Dec. 1 stitch in every cable as follows: *P1, S1, K2, PSSO; Rep. from * to last stitch, P1.

Next Row *K1, P2, Rep. from * to last stitch, K1. Cast off.

Join left shoulder seam and neckband.

Single thickness neckband.

Double thickness neckband.

Double-thickness neckband

Starting with Row 3 of cable pattern, work until 3 cable rows have been completed.
Change to size 2.25 mm needles.

Work in pattern until 4 cable rows have been completed then work a further 3 rows.

Next Cable Row Dec. 1 stitch in every cable as follows: *P1, S1, K2, PSSO;
Rep. from * to last stitch, P1.

Next Row   (K1, P2) Rep. to last stitch, K1.

Next Row   (P1, K2) Rep. to last stitch, P1.

Next Row   (K1, P2) Rep. to last stitch, K1.

Next Row   (P1, S1, inc. in next stitch, PSSO and knit) Rep. to last stitch, P1.

Continue in pattern until 7 cable rows have been completed then work Row 4.

Change back to size 2.75 mm needles and continue in pattern until 10 cable rows
in all have been completed.

Next Row

1st Size   P5, P2 tog., (P4, P2 tog.) 26 times, P6. 169 sts.

2nd & 3rd Sizes P3, P2 tog., (P4, P2 tog.) 28 times, P4. 177 sts.

4th & 5th Sizes P1, P2 tog., (P4, P2 tog.) 30 times, P2. 185 sts.

6th Size   P2, P2 tog., (P4, P2 tog.) 31 times, P3. 193 sts.

Cast off on size 3 mm needles. Join left shoulder seam and neckband.

Fold neckband in half and stitch cast-off edge to pick-up edge on wrong side.

Alternative round neckbands for Jumper, Tunic or Dress

These neckbands are joined to the jumper after they have been knitted.

Double-thickness neckband (Cable front with stocking stitch back)

Method of casting on

Two-needle method. Make a loop on the left-hand needle, insert right-hand needle
into this loop and pull yarn through placing this on to the left-hand needle to form
a stitch. *Insert right-hand needle in between the first two stitches on left-hand
needle and pull yarn through to form a new stitch. Repeat from * until required
number of stitches have been cast on.

Cast on 142 (148; 148; 154; 154; 161) sts. on size 3.25 mm needles.

Change to size 2.75 mm needles and increase as follows:

1st Size   K6, Up1, (K5, Up1) 26 times, K6. 169 sts.

2nd & 3rd Sizes K4, Up1, (K5, Up1) 28 times, K4. 177 sts.

4th & 5th Sizes K2, Up1, (K5, Up1) 30 times, K2. 185 sts.

6th Size   K3, Up1, (K5, Up1) 31 times, K3. 193 sts. ***

Starting with Row 2 of cable pattern (see p. 67) work 11 rows, then change to size 2.25 mm needles and work Rows 1 and 2 of cable pattern.

Next Row Dec. 1 stitch in every cable as follows: P1, *S1, K2, PSSO, P1.
              Rep. from * to end.

Next Row K1, (P2, K1) to end.

Next Row P1, (K2, P1) to end.

Next Row K1, (P2, K1) to end.

Next Row Knit, increasing evenly to 142 (148; 148; 154; 154; 161) sts.

Work 5 rows in stocking stitch starting with purl row.

Change to size 2.75 mm needles and continue in stocking stitch for 11 more rows, ending with a knit row.

Make a tube by knitting one stitch from caston edge with 1 stitch from needle. Leave stitches on needle for join without backstitch, or transfer stitches on to holder for backstitch join.

Join right shoulder seam. With Size 2.75 mm. Needle pick up stitches around neck as follows: With right side facing pick up 13 (14; 14; 15; 15; 16) sts. down straight of left front neck, 23 sts.down curve, 19 (21; 21; 23; 23; 25) sts. across front (cast off sts.) 23 sts. up curve of right front neck, and 13 (14; 14; 15; 15; 16) sts. up straight of right front neck, 4 sts. down curve of right back neck, 43 (45; 45; 47; 47; 50) sts. across back (cast off sts.) and 4 sts. up curve of left back neck. 142 (148; 148; 154; 154; 161) sts.

Join neckband to jumper as follows
Join without backstitching After picking up stitches around neck, knit 1 row. With right sides together, join neckband to jumper and knit 1 row by working 1 stitch from neckband together with 1 stitch from jumper, **at same time** cast off stitches while working across row. Join left shoulder seam and neckband.

Double thickness neckband without backstitch.

Double thickness neckband with backstitch.

Backstitch decorative join

With wrong side of jumper and right side of neckband facing you (i.e. wrong sides together) and neckband nearest to you, knit 1 row by working 1 stitch from neckband together with one stitch from jumper.

Purl 1 row and knit 1 row.

Place stitches on thread. Join left shoulder and neckband.

Backstitch the stitches on thread evenly around neck of jumper. Remove thread.

Single-thickness neckband

Work as for Double Neckband to *** p. 70)

Work cable pattern (see p. 67) starting with Row 2, until 3 cable rows have been worked. Work 3 rows in pattern.

Change to size 2.25 mm needles and work 4 more rows in pattern.

Next Row Decrease in every cable as follows: (P1, S1, K2, PSSO) to last stitch, P1.

Next Row *K1, P2, Rep. from * to last stitch, K1. Cast off in pattern.

Pick up stitches around neck following instructions for double neckband.

Leave these stitches on needle.

Single thickness neckband without backstitch.

Single thickness neckband with backstitch.

Join neckband to jumper as follows:

Join without backstitching After picking up stitches around neck, knit 1 row. With right sides together, pick up 1 stitch from *cast-on* edge of neckband with 1 stitch from needle on jumper and knit together, *at the same time* cast off stitches while working across row. Join left shoulder seam and neckband.

Backstitch decorative join With wrong side of jumper and right side of neckband facing you (i.e. wrong sides together) and neckband nearest to you, pick up 1 stitch from *cast-on* edge of neckband with 1 stitch from needle on jumper and knit together. Purl 1 row then knit 1 row.

Place stitches on thread. Join left shoulder seam and neckband.

Backstitch the stitches on thread evenly around neck of jumper. Remove thread.

Neckband for V-neck Jumper, Tunic or Dress

(Size 2.75 mm needles)

Join left shoulder seam. Pick up stitches around neck as follows:

With right side facing, pick up 5 sts. down curve of right back neck, 43 (45; 45; 47; 47; 49) sts. across cast-off stitches, 5 sts. up curve of left back neck; 105 (109; 109; 113; 113; 117) sts. down left front neck, pick up centre stitch, then 105 (109; 109; 113; 113; 117) sts. up right front neck.

Next Row (K1, P3) to last stitch before centre stitch, K1; Purl centre stitch; K1, (P3, K1) to shoulder seam; increase 11 (13; 13; 15; 15; 17) sts. evenly across back neck to 64 (68; 68; 72; 72; 76) sts. as follows:

1st Size Inc. in 4th and 5th sts. alternately to last 8 sts., P4, inc. in next st., P3.

2nd and 3rd Sizes Inc. in every 4th stitch until last 3 sts., P3.

4th and 5th Sizes Inc. in every 4th and 3rd sts. alternately to last 8 sts. P3, inc. in next st., P4.

6th Size (P2, inc. in next st., P3, inc. in next st.) 3 times; (P2, inc. in next st.) 5 times; (P2, inc. in next st., P3, inc. in next st.) 3 times; P2.

Total 275 (287; 287; 299; 299; 311) sts.

Next Row Work Row 3 of cable pattern (see p. 67) to last 4sts. before centre stitch of V neck. S1, K2, PSSO, P1, K1, P1, S1, K2, PSSO; pattern to end.

Next Row Pattern to last 2 sts. before centre stitch, P2 tog., P1, P2 tog. tbl., P1, pattern to end.

Next Row Pattern to last 2 sts. before centre stitch, S1, K1, PSSO, K1, K2 tog., pattern to end.

Next Row Pattern to last 2 sts. before centre stitch, S1, K1, PSSO, P1, K2 tog., pattern to end.

Repeat last 4 rows.

Next Row (P1, S1, K2, PSSO) to last 5 sts. before centre stitch, P1, S1, K2, PSSO, P1, K1, P1, S1, K2, PSSO, P1, pattern to end.

V neck neckband.

Next Row (K1, P2) to last 4 sts. before centre stitch, K1, P1, P2 tog., P1, P2 tog. tbl., P1, K1. (P2, K1) to end.

Cast off in pattern to last 2 sts. before centre stitch. Continue casting off the next 5 sts. working as follows: S1, K1, PSSO, K1, K2 tog. Cast off in pattern to end.
Join right shoulder seam and neckband.

Bottom band for Jumper, Tunic or Dress

With right side facing, place panels and bands on to a size 2.75 mm circular needle in the following order. Right to left.

Back Left Side Band

Back Panel

Back Right Side Band

Right Side Panel

Front Right Side Band

Front Panel

Front Left Side Band

Left Side Panel

Working backwards and forwards on circular needle and starting with right side facing, work across panels and bands as follows:

Cable Bands P2 tog., pattern to last 2 sts., P2 tog.

All Stocking Stitch Panels apart from Left Side Panel:

K2 tog., K1, inc. in next st,. * K2, inc. in next stitch, Rep. from * to last 4 sts., K2, S1, K1, PSSO.

Left Side Panel

K2 tog., K1, inc. in next st., *K2, inc. in next stitch, Rep. from * to last 4 sts., K4.

Next Row K1, *P3, K1, Rep. from * to end.

Continue in cable pattern beginning with Row 3 until 6 cable rows have been completed and work Rows 4, 1 and 2 again.

Next Row P1, *S1, K2, PSSO and knit, P1, S1, K2, PSSO, P1; Rep. from * to end.

Next Row Work in pattern as set.

Cast off in pattern.

Button and buttonhole bands for round-neck Jacket or Waistcoat

Button band (**Size 3mm needles**)

This band is worked from the top downwards.

CABLE PATTERN

Row 1 P2, (K3, P1) 4 times, P1.

Row 2 K2, (P3, K1) 4 times, K1.

Row 3 P2, (S1, K2, PSSO and *at the same time knit into slip stitch*, P1) 4 times, P1.

Row 4 As Row 2.

With waste yarn cast on 19 sts. and work 5 rows in stocking stitch.

Change to main yarn and work Row 4 of cable pattern.

Continue in pattern until 217 (217; 217; 213; 213; 213) rows (short length), 253 (253; 253; 249; 249; 249) rows (medium length) and 289 (289; 289; 285; 285; 285) rows (long length) have been completed, ending on Row 4. 54 (54; 54; 53; 53; 53) cables (short length); 63 (63; 63; 62; 62; 62) cables (medium length); 72 (72; 72; 71; 71; 71) cables (long length).

Leave stitches on holder for bottom band. Remove waste yarn and carefully place 19 sts. of first row of main yarn on to holder.

Buttonhole band

(**Size 3mm needles**)

This band is worked from the top downwards.

Short Length Jacket has 9 buttonholes: 1 in neckband, 6 in front band and 2 in bottom band.

Buttonhole band.

Medium and Long Length Jackets have 5 buttonholes: 1 in neckband, 4 in front band.

CABLE PATTERN

Row 1 P2, (K3, P1) 4 times, P1.

Row 2 K2, (P3, K1) 4 times K1.

Row 3 P2, (S1, K2, PSSO and *at the same time knit into slip stitch*, P1) 4 times, P1.

Row 4 As Row 2.

Short length (button-through)

With waste yarn cast on 19 sts. and work 4 rows in stocking stitch.

Change to main yarn and beginning with Row 1:

** Work 4-row cable pattern 6 times for first three sizes and 5 times for last three sizes.

Work buttonhole in next 7 rows beginning in Row 1 as follows:

P1, (P1, K3) twice, inc. in next stitch, (K3, P1) twice, P1.

Next Row K2, (P3, K1) twice, turn.

Work cable pattern for 4 rows on these 10 sts., leaving 10 sts. on other needle.

Break off yarn and rejoin to remaining 10 sts.

Work 5 rows of pattern on these 10 sts.

Next Row P1, (P1, S1, K2, PSSO and knit) twice,

P2 tog., (S1, K2, PSSO and knit, P1) twice, P1.

Work Row 4 of cable pattern.

First 3 Sizes

Repeat from ** 5 times.

Work 4-row cable pattern 6 times. (216 rows in all)

Leave stitches on holder for bottom band.

Last 3 sizes

*** Work 4-row cable pattern 6 times.

Work 7 rows of buttonhole.

Work Row 4 of cable pattern.

Repeat from *** 4 times.

Work 4-row cable pattern 6 times (212 rows in all).

Leave stitches on holder for bottom band.

Medium and long lengths (all sizes)

With waste yarn cast on 19 sts. and work 4 rows in stocking stitch.

Change to main yarn and beginning with Row 1:

** Work 4-row cable pattern 6 times.

Work 7 rows of buttonhole as for short length.

Work Row 4 of cable pattern. Repeat from ** 3 times.

Work in pattern until 252 (252; 252; 248; 248; 248) rows (medium length) and 288 (288; 288; 284; 284; 284) rows (long length) are completed.

Leave stitches on holder for bottom band.

Remove waste yarn and carefully place 19 sts. of first row of main yarn on to holder.

Neckband for round-neck jacket or waistcoat
(Size 2.75mm needles)

CABLE PATTERN

Row 1 P2, *K3, P1, Rep. from * to last stitch, P1.

Row 2 K2, *P3, K1, Rep. from * to last stitch, K1.

Row 3 P2, *S1, K2, PSSO and *at the same time knit into slip stitch,* P1.
Rep. from * to last stitch, P1.

Row 4 As Row 2.

Join shoulder seams.

Place stitches of buttonhole band on to needle and, with wrong side facing, K2, (P3, K1) 4 times, K1.

Next Row Work across buttonhole band (first row of buttonhole) as follows: P2, K3, P1, K3. Inc. in next st., K3, P1, K3, P2 tog. then pick up stitches around neckband as follows: Pick up 27 (28; 27; 30; 29; 30) sts. up curve of right front, 7 (8; 9; 9; 10; 11) sts. up straight of right front, 4 sts. down curve of right back neck, 43 (45; 45; 47; 47; 49) sts. across cast-off stitches and 4 sts. up curve of left back neck, 7 (8; 9; 9; 10; 11) sts. down straight of left front and 27 (28; 27; 30; 29; 30) sts.

down curve of left front, then work across button band, right side facing, as follows:
P2 tog., (K3, P1) 4 times, P1. 156 (162; 162; 170; 170; 176) sts.

Next Row Work across button band then increase to last 19 sts. of buttonhole band as follows:

1st Size (P2, inc. in next stitch by purling into front and knitting into back, P3, K1) 8 times; (P3, K1) twice; (P2, inc. in next stitch, P3, K1) 7 times; P2, inc. in next stitch, P3.

2nd, 3rd & 6th Sizes (P2, inc. in next stitch by purling into front and knitting into back, P3, K1) to last 6 sts. P2, inc. in next stitch, P3.

4th & 5th Sizes (P2, inc. in next stitch by purling into front and knitting into back, P3, K1) 9 times; (P3, K1) twice; (P2, inc. in next stitch, P3, K1) 8 times; P2, inc. in next stitch, P3.

Continue across buttonhole band as follows: K1, P3, K1, P3, K1, turn, leaving 10 sts. on other needle. 171 (179; 179; 187; 187; 195) sts. in all (not counting extra buttonhole stitch).
Continue in pattern across neckband working buttonhole in next 5 rows as before.

Single-thickness neckband

Continue in pattern until 5 cable rows have been completed then change to size 2.25 mm needles and work a further 3 rows.

Next Cable Row Dec. 1 stitch in every cable as follows: P1, *P1, S1, K2, PSSO; Rep. from * to last 2 stitches, P2.

Next Row K1 *K1, P2, Rep. from * to last 2 stitches, K2. Cast off.

Double-thickness neckband

Continue in pattern until 3 cable rows have been completed then change to size 2.25 mm needles.
Work in pattern until 4 cable rows have been completed then work a further 3 rows.

Single thickness neckband for jacket.

Double thickness neckband for jacket.

Next Cable Row Dec. 1 stitch in every cable as follows: P1, *P1, S1, K2, PSSO; Rep. from * to last 2 stitches, P2.

Next Row K1, (K1, P2) to last 2 stitches, K2.

Next Row P1, (P1, K2) to last 2 stitches, P2.

Next Row K1, (K1, P2) to last 2 stitches, K2.

Next Row P1, (P1, S1,inc. in next stitch, PSSO and knit) to last 2 stitches, P2.

Work Row 4.

Change back to size 2.75 mm needles and continue in pattern until 8 cable rows in all have been completed then work Row 4.

Work a further buttonhole in next 7 rows, beginning with Row 1 and ending with Row 3.

Next Row Work across 18 sts. of button band then decrease to last 18 sts. of buttonhole band as follows:

1st Size (P2, K2 tog., P3, K1) 8 times; (P3, K1) twice; (P2, K2 tog., P3, K1) 7 times; P2, K2 tog., P3.

2nd, 3rd, & 6th Sizes (P2, K2 tog., P3, K1) to last 7 sts., P2, K2 tog., P3.

4th & 5th Sizes (P2, K2 tog., P3, K1) 9 times; (P3, K1) twice; (P2, K2 tog., P3, K1) 8 times; P2, K2 tog., P3.

Continue across buttonhole band in pattern.

155 (161; 161; 169; 169; 175) sts.

Cast off on size 3 mm needle.

Fold neckband in half, stitch cast-off edge to pick-up edge on wrong side.

Join front edges of neckband together.

Button and buttonhole bands for V-neck jacket or waistcoat

These bands are worked from the top downwards and joined at the centre back neck.

Button band

CABLE PATTERN

Row 1 P2, (K3, P1) 4 times, P1.

Row 2 K2, (P3, K1) 4 times, K1.

Row 3 P2, (S1, K2, PSSO and *at the same time knit into slip stitch,* P1)
4 times, P1.

Row 4 As Row 2.

With waste yarn cast on 19 sts. and work 5 rows in stocking stitch.

Change to main yarn and work Row 4 of cable pattern.

Continue in pattern until 72 (81; 90) cables are completed, 289 (325; 361) rows.

First figure for short length, figures in brackets for medium and long lengths respectively.

Leave stitches on holder for bottom band.

Work a further 4 rows on this button band only, for the last 3 sizes, to allow for the larger size back neck.

Buttonhole band

Remove waste yarn from button band and place 19 stitches of first row of main yarn on to needle.

CABLE PATTERN

Work as for button band.

With right side facing, rejoin main yarn and starting with Row 1 continue in pattern until 37 cables for Sizes 1 & 2; 39 cables for Sizes 3 & 4; and 41 cables for Sizes 5 & 6 are completed.

**Work buttonhole in next 7 rows beginning in Row 1 as follows:

P1, (P1, K3) twice, inc. in next stitch, (K3, P1) twice, P1.

Next Row K2, (P3, K1) twice, turn.

Work cable pattern for 4 rows on these 10 sts., leaving 10 sts. on other needle.

Break off yarn and rejoin to remaining 10 sts.

Work 5 rows of pattern on these 10 sts.

Next Row P1, (P1, S1, K2, PSSO and knit) twice, P2 tog., (S1, K2, PSSO and knit, P1) twice, P1.

Work Row 4 of cable pattern.

Short Length

Sizes 1 & 2

Work 4-row cable pattern 5 times. ***

Repeat from ** to *** 4 times. 288 rows.

Leave stitches on holder for bottom band.

Sizes 3 & 4

Work 26 rows of cable pattern.

Work buttonhole in next 7 rows starting on Row 3 of cable pattern.

Work 25 rows of cable pattern.

Work buttonhole in next 7 rows starting on Row 3 of cable pattern.

Work 27 rows of cable pattern.

Work buttonhole in next 7 rows starting on Row 1 of cable pattern.

Work 25 rows of cable pattern. 288 rows.

Leave stitches on holder for bottom band.

Sizes 5 & 6

Work 22 rows of cable pattern.

Work buttonhole in next 7 rows starting on Row 3 of cable pattern.

Work 25 rows of cable pattern.

Work buttonhole in next 7 rows starting on Row 3 of cable pattern.

Work 23 rows of cable pattern.

Work buttonhole in next 7 rows starting on Row 1 of cable pattern.

Work 25 rows of cable pattern. 288 rows.

Leave stitches on holder for bottom band.

Medium & long lengths (these have only 4 buttonholes)

Work 4-row cable pattern 6 times. ****

Repeat from ** to **** 3 times.

Continue in cable pattern until 324 rows (medium length) and 360 rows (long length).

Leave stitches on holder for bottom band.

Bottom band for Jacket or Waistcoat
(short length, button-through)

There is a choice of two lengths of band, one with two buttonholes (8 cables) and one with one buttonhole (5 cables).

With right side facing, place panels and bands on to a size 2.75 mm circular needle in the following order. Right to left.

Button Band

Left Front

Left Front Side Band

Left Side Panel

Left Back Side Band

Back Panel

Right Back Side Band

Right Side Panel

Right Front Side Band

Right Front

Buttonhole Band

Working backwards and forwards on circular needle and starting with right side facing, work across panels and bands as follows:

Left front band

Pattern across first 17 sts. of band then P2 tog.

All stocking stitch panels

K2 tog., K1, inc. in next st., *K2, inc. in next st., Rep. from * to last 4 sts. K2, S1, K1, PSSO.

Side bands

P2 tog., pattern to last 2 sts., P2 tog. **

Right front band

First Buttonhole Row P2 tog., K3, P1, K3, inc. in next stitch, (K3, P1) twice, P1.

Bottom band (8 cables)

Next Row K2, (P3, K1) twice, turn.

Work cable pattern for 4 rows on these 10 sts.

Break off yarn and rejoin to remaining sts. K1, (P3, K1) twice, K1.

Work 4 more rows in pattern.

Next Row

(last buttonhole row) Work across all sts. in pattern to last 11 sts.

P2 tog., (S1, K2, PSSO and knit, P1) twice, P1.

Work Row 4 of cable pattern. #

Work 4-row cable pattern 3 times and work buttonhole in next 7 rows as before.

Work Rows 4, 1 and 2 of cable pattern again.

Next Row

(cable row) Dec. in every other cable as follows: P1, *P1, S1, K2, PSSO and knit; P1, S1, K2, PSSO; Rep. from * to last 2 sts., P2.

Work 1 row in pattern as set. Cast off in pattern.

Bottom band (5 cables)

Work as for pattern for 8 cables to #, then work 7 rows in cable pattern.

Omit last buttonhole and continue from ##.

Bottom band for Jacket or Waistcoat
(Medium and long length, no buttonhole in bottom band).
Work as for short length to **

Right front band
P2 tog., pattern to end.

Bottom band (5 cables)
Next Row Work Row 2 of cable pattern.

Work in pattern until 4 cable rows have been completed and work Rows 4, 1 and 2 again.

Next Row (cable row) Dec. in every other cable as follows: P1, *P1, S1, K2, PSSO
and knit; P1, S1, K2, PSSO; Rep. from * to last 2 sts., P2.

Work 1 row in pattern as set. Cast off in pattern.

Band on top of straight side panels for sleeveless top
(Size 2.75 mm needles)
With right side of work facing, pick up 46 (49; 52; 55; 58; 61) sts. across top of side panel.

Purl 1 row as follows: K1, *P2, increase in next stitch by purling into front and then
knitting into back of stitch. Rep. from * to end.

Work in pattern, beginning with Row 3, and continue in pattern for 12 rows
ending on Row 2.

Next Row Decrease one stitch in every cable as follows: P1, *S1, K2, PSSO, P1,
Rep. from * to end.

Next Row K1, *P2, K1, Rep. from * to end. Cast off.

Band on top of flared side panels for sleeveless top
(Size 2.75 mm needles)
With right side of work facing, pick up 48 (51; 54; 57; 60; 63) sts. across top of side panel.

Purl 1 row as follows: Inc. in first stitch by purling into front and then knitting
into back of stitch, P1, inc. in next stitch then every 3rd stitch to end. Work in pattern,
beginning with Row 3, and continue in pattern for 12 rows ending on Row 2.

Next Row Decrease 1 stitch in every cable as follows: P1, *SI, K2, PSSO, P1, Rep. from * to end.

Next Row K1, *P2,K1, Rep. from * to end. Cast off.

Bands for cape sleeves

(Size 2.75mm circular needle, working backwards and forwards)

CABLE PATTERN

Row 1 P1, *K3, P1, Rep. from * to end.

Row 2 K1, *P3, K1, Rep. from * to end.

Row 3 P1, *S1, K2, PSSO, and *at the same time knit into slip stitch,* P1.
   Rep. from * to end.

Row 4 As Row 2.

Starting with right side facing, pick up stitches between markers as follows:

28 to first marker.

27 between 1st and 2nd marker.

32 between 2nd and 3rd marker.

45 between 3rd and 4th marker.

34 between 4th and 5th marker.

16 between 5th and 6th marker.

18 between 6th and 7th marker.

17 between 7th and 8th marker.

15 between 8th and 9th marker.

11 between 9th and 10th marker.

16 between 10th and 11th marker at centre of cape sleeve. (259 sts.)

Next Row K1 *P2, inc. in next stitch (by purling into front and knitting into back),
   Rep. from * to end. (345 sts.)

Starting with Row 3 of cable pattern (right side), continue in pattern until two
cable rows have been completed and then work Rows 4, 1 and 2 again.

Next Row Decrease 1 stitch in every cable as follows: P1, *SI, K2, PSSO, P1,
   Rep. from * to end.

Next Row K1, *P2, K1, Rep. from * to end. Cast off.

Work remaining piece picking up stitches in reverse order.

Join seam in centre.

Straight Skirt

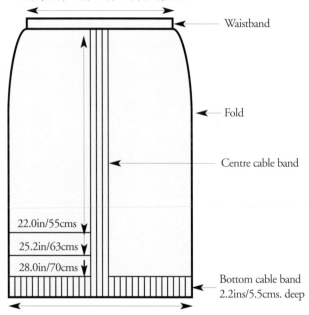

16.2in (17.0in, 17.8in, 18.6in, 19.4in, 20.2in)
40.5 (42.5, 44.5, 46.5, 48.5, 50.5) cms

→ Waistband

← Fold

← Centre cable band

22.0in/55cms

25.2in/63cms

28.0in/70cms

← Bottom cable band
2.2ins/5.5cms. deep

19.4in (20.2in, 21.0in, 21.8in, 22.6in, 23.4in)
48.5 (50.5, 52.5, 54.5, 56.5, 58.5) cms
Total of one panel and one band

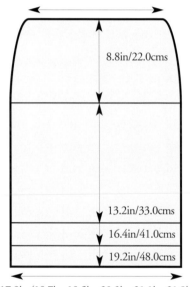

14.7in (15.5in, 16.3in, 17.1in, 17.9in, 18.7in)
36.8 (38.8, 40.8, 42.8, 44.8, 46.8,) cms

8.8in/22.0cms

13.2in/33.0cms

16.4in/41.0cms

19.2in/48.0cms

17.9in (18.7in, 19.5in, 20.3in, 21.1in, 21.9in)
44.8 (46.8, 48.8, 50.8, 52.8, 54.8) cms
The decreasing from hip to waist is in the centre of
panel not on the edge as shown

Straight skirt (*Hand or machine*)

NOTES * Shorten or lengthen in multiples of 4 rows and
adjust number of cables on centre bands accordingly,
i.e. 1 cable = 4 rows. The width can be altered in
multiples of 6 sts.

** Fully fashioned method decrease.

*Jumper with swiss
darned embroidery
on front; straight
skirt.*

Machine Knit Using 2-hook transfer needle, take off centre 2 stitches. Using 1-hook transfer needle move 1 stitch from either side on to empty centre needles. Replace 2 stitches from 2-hook transfer needle. Transfer all remaining stitches 1 stitch towards centre.

Hand Knit S1, K1, PSSO, K2 tog.

Panels – work 2

With waste yarn cast on 134 (140; 146; 152; 158; 164) sts. and work 4 rows in stocking stitch.

With main yarn work 132 rows in stocking stitch for short length, 164 rows for medium length and 192 rows for long length. Adjust length here if required (see note *).

Next Row Dec. 2 sts. in centre using fully fashioned method (see note**) on next and every following 8th row 10 times

(11 decrease rows in all).

Work 6 rows without shaping then work 1 row decreasing 1 stitch at each end. 110 (116; 122; 128; 134; 140) sts.

220 rows for short length, 252 rows for medium length and 280 rows for long length. Leave stitches on holder for waistband.

Remove waste yarn and place first row of main yarn on to holder.

Skirt panel.

Centre cable bands – work 2

These bands are worked from the top downwards.

With waste yarn cast on 19 sts. and work 4 rows in stocking stitch.

Change to main yarn.

CABLE PATTERN

Row 1 P1, (P1, K3) 4 times, P2.

Row 2 K1, (K1, P3) 4 times, K2.

Row 3 P1, (P1, S1, K2, PSSO and *at the same time knit into slip stitch*)
4 times, P2.

Row 4 As Row 2.

These 4 rows form 1 cable. Repeat until 55 cables for short length, 63 cables for medium length and 70 cables for long length have been completed. Decrease 1 stitch at each end of last row (Row 4). 17 sts. Leave stitches on holder for bottom band. Remove waste yarn and carefully place 19 sts. of first row of main yarn on to holder.

Waistband

With right side facing, work across 110 (116; 122; 128; 134; 140) sts. of left side panel as follows: Inc. in first stitch, P1, (K1, P1) to last stitch; work across 19 sts. of centre front band as follows: K2 tog., work in rib to last 2 sts., K2 tog.; continue in P1, K1 rib working across the 110 (116; 122; 128; 134; 140) sts. of right side panel; work in rib across 19 sts. of centre back band, decreasing one stitch at each end. 255 (267; 279; 291; 303; 315) sts.

Full skirt, front view.

Work a further 15 rows in K1, P1 rib, followed by 16 rows of stocking stitch. Cast off loosely.

Bottom cable band

CABLE PATTERN

Row 1 P1, *K3, P1, Rep. from * to end.

Row 2 K1, *P3, K1, Rep. from * to end.

Row 3 P1, *S1, K2, PSSO *at the same time knit into slip stitch,* P1. Rep. from *
to end.

Row 4 As Row 2.

With right side facing, work in pattern across centre back band starting with Row 1 then work across stitches of right side panel as follows: K2 tog., K1, inc. in next stitch, *K2, inc. in next st. Rep from * to last 4 sts., K2, S1, K1, PSSO; work in pattern across centre front band then across stitches of left side panel as instructed for right side panel to last 4 sts., K3, P1.

Next Row K1, *P3, K1, Rep. from * to end.

Continue in cable pattern beginning with Row 3 until 5 cable rows have been completed and work Rows 4, 1 and 2 again.

Next Row P1, *S1, K2, PSSO and knit, P1; S1, K2, PSSO, P1;
Rep. from * to end.

Next Row Work in pattern as set.

Cast off in pattern.

Finishing

Sew in cable bands with mattress stitch, row for row.

Fold over 16 rows of stocking stitch on waistband and fasten down to bottom of rib on wrong side. Insert 1in Peta-stretch elastic to required length.

Gored Skirt

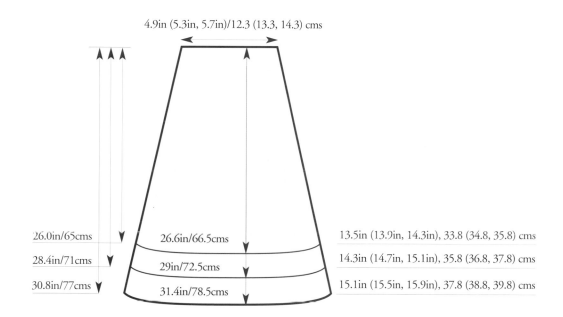

4.9in (5.3in, 5.7in)/12.3 (13.3, 14.3) cms

26.0in/65cms

28.4in/71cms

30.8in/77cms

26.6in/66.5cms

29in/72.5cms

31.4in/78.5cms

13.5in (13.9in, 14.3in), 33.8 (34.8, 35.8) cms

14.3in (14.7in, 15.1in), 35.8 (36.8, 37.8) cms

15.1in (15.5in, 15.9in), 37.8 (38.8, 39.8) cms

Gored panel (*Machine knit – work 6*)

* NOTE Increase by transferring end stitch on left-hand side, one needle to left, and taking loop under second stitch from left side on to empty needle, then transferring end stitch on right-hand side, one needle to right, and taking loop under second stitch from right side on to empty needle and work across all stitches.

Push forward into working position 37 (40, 43), needles in centre of needle bed.
Work a few rows on waste yarn ending with carriage on right.
Change to main yarn and set row counter to 000. Work 4 rows.

91

Increase * (see note) at each end of next and every following 8th row until:

101 (104; 107)sts. short length

107 (110; 113)sts. medium length

113 (116; 119)sts. long length

Work a further 7 rows

260 rows short length; 284 rows medium length; 308 rows long length.

Short length

Cast off 12 (12; 13)sts. at beginning and 1 stitch at end of next 2 rows.

Cast off 11 (12; 12)sts. at beginning and 1 stitch at end of next 2 rows.

Cast off 12 (12; 12)sts. at beginning and 1 stitch at end of next 2 rows.

Cast off remaining 25 (26; 27)sts. (266 rows)

Medium length

Cast off 13 (13; 13) sts. at beginning and 1 stitch at end of next 2 rows.

Cast off 12 (12; 13)sts. at beginning and 1 stitch at end of next 2 rows.

Cast off 12 (13; 13)sts. at beginning and 1 stitch at end of next 2 rows.

Cast off remaining 27 (28; 29)sts. (290 rows)

Long length

Cast off 13 (14; 14)sts. at beginning and 1 stitch at end of next 2 rows.

Cast off 13 (13; 13)sts. at beginning and 1 stitch at end of next 2 rows.

Cast off 13 (13; 14)sts. at beginning and 1 stitch at end of next 2 rows.

Cast off remaining 29 (30; 31)sts. (314 rows)

Remove waste yarn and place stitches on holder for waist rib.

Gored panel (*Hand knit – work 6*)

* NOTE Increase at beginning of row by pulling up loop in between first two stitches and knitting into back of it. Increase at end of row by pulling up loop in between last two stitches and knitting into back of it.

V-neck waistcoat and gored skirt.

Cast on 37 (40, 43) sts. and work a few rows on waste yarn ending with a purl row.

Change to main yarn and work 4 rows.

Increase (see note *) at each end of next and every following 8th row until:

101 (104; 107) sts. – short length, 107 (110; 113) sts. – medium length,

113 (116; 119) sts. – long length.

Work a further 7 rows.

260 rows – short length; 284 rows – medium length; 308 rows – long length.

** NOTE Shaping bottom of skirt panel by turning without leaving holes.

(a) Knit Row:

Bring yarn to front of work and slip next stitch from LH to RH needle.

Return yarn to back of work and return slipped stitch to LH needle.

(b) Purl Row:

Place yarn to back of work and slip next stitch from LH to RH needle.

Return yarn to front of work and return slipped stitch to LH needle.

(c) Knit Row:

Slip the next stitch from LH to RH needle at the same time lifting the loop around it up on to the RH needle making an extra stitch.

Replace the 2 sts. on to the LH needle and knit them together.

(d) Purl Row:

Slip the next stitch from LH to RH needle at the same time lifting the loop around it up on to the RH needle making an extra stitch.

Replace the 2 sts. on to the LH needle and purl them together by purling into front of 2nd stitch, then into the back of 1st stitch.

Short length

Knit to last 13 (13; 14)sts., work (a), turn,

Purl to last 13 (13; 14)sts., work (b), turn,

Knit to last 25 (26; 27)sts., work (a), turn,

Purl to last 25 (26; 27)sts., work (b), turn,

Knit to last 38 (39; 40)sts., work (a), turn,

Purl to last 38 (39; 40)sts., work (b), turn,

Next Row K25 (26; 27) sts., work (c); K12 (12; 12) sts., work (c);
K11 (12; 12) sts., work (c); K12 (12; 13) sts.

Next Row P63 (65; 67)sts., work (d); P12 (12; 12)sts. work (d);
P11 (12; 12) sts., work (d); P12 (12; 13) sts. 268 rows.

Medium length

Knit to last 14 (14; 14)sts., work (a), turn,

Purl to last 14 (14; 14)sts., work (b), turn,

Knit to last 27 (27; 28)sts., work (a), turn,

Purl to last 27 (27; 28)sts., work (b), turn,

Knit to last 40 (41; 42)sts., work (a), turn,

Purl to last 40 (41; 42)sts., work (b), turn,

Next Row K27 (28; 29)sts., work (c); K12 (13; 13) sts., work (c);
K12 (12; 13)sts.,work (c); K13 (13; 13)sts.

Next Row P67 (69; 71)sts., work (d); P12 (13; 13)sts., work (d);
P12 (12; 13)sts., work (d); P13 (13; 13) sts. 292 Rows.

Long length

Knit to last 14 (15; 15)sts., work (a), turn,

Purl to last 14 (15; 15)sts., work (b), turn,

Knit to last 28 (29; 29)sts., work (a), turn,

Purl to last 28 (29; 29)sts., work (b), turn,

Knit to last 42 (43; 44)sts., work (a), turn,

Purl to last 42 (43; 44)sts., work (b), turn,

Next Row K29 (30; 31)sts., work (c); K13 (13; 14)sts., work (c);
K13 (13; 13)sts., work (c); K13 (14; 14)sts.

Next Row P71 (73; 75)sts., work (d); P13 (13; 14)sts., work (d);
P13 (13; 13)sts., work (d); P13 (14; 14)sts. 316 rows.

Place stitches on holder. Remove waste yarn and place stitches on
holder for waist rib.

Mock cable bands (work 6)

These bands are worked from the top downwards.

CABLE PATTERN

Row 1 P1, (P1, K3) 4 times, P2.

Row 2 K1, (K1, P3) 4 times, K2.

Row 3 P1, (P1, S1, K2, PSSO *and at the same time knit into slip stitch)*
4 times, P2.

Row 4 As Row 2.

With waste yarn cast on 19 sts. and work 4 rows in stocking stitch.

Change to main yarn and work cable pattern starting with Row 1 for:

260 rows (65 cables) short length.

284 rows (71 cables) medium length.

308 rows (77 cables) long length.

Leave sts. on holder for bottom band.

Remove waste yarn and carefully place 19 sts. of first row of main yarn on to holder for waist rib.

Sew in cable bands between panels with mattress stitch, row for row, leaving 1 seam open between panel on left and cable band on right.

Waist rib

Right side facing, work across panels and cable bands alternately as follows:

First panel P1, *K10 (11; 12), K2 tog. Rep. from * once,
K10 (11; 12), S1, K1, PSSO.

All cable bands P2 tog., *K2, S1, P1, PSSO. Rep. from * twice, K2, S1, P2 tog., PSSO.

Remaining panels K2 tog., K10 (11; 12), K2 tog., K9 (10; 11), K2 tog.,
K10 (11; 12), S1, K1, PSSO. 277 (295; 314) sts.

Next Row K1, P1, to last stitch, K1.

Work a further 15 rows in rib followed by 16 rows of stocking stitch.

Cast off loosely.

Bottom band

CABLE PATTERN

Row 1 P1, *K3, P1, Rep. from * to end.

Row 2 K1, *P3, K1, Rep. from * to end.

Row 3 P1, *S1, K2, PSSO, *at the same time knit into slip stitch*, P1.
Rep. from * to end.

Row 4 As Row 2.

Detail of gored skirt.

With circular needle working backwards and forwards, starting with cable band work around bottom three panels, right side facing, as follows:

Cable bands

P2 tog., pattern to last 2 sts., P2 tog.

Stocking stitch panels: Hand-knitted

Knit the first two and last two stitches of each panel together. These are used in the sewing up.

348 (357; 366) sts. – short length, 366 (375; 384) sts. – medium length, 384 (393; 402) sts. – long length.

Stocking stitch panels: Machine-knitted

Pick up 99 (102; 105) sts. for short length, 105 (108; 111) sts. for medium length, and 111 (114; 117) sts. for long length, by omitting the first and last stitch in each panel which is used in the sewing up.

348 (357; 366) sts. – short length, 366 (375; 384) sts. – medium length, 384 (393; 402) sts. – long length.

Continue band for either, as follows:

Next Row Inc. in 1st stitch by purling into front and then knitting into back of stitch, P1, inc. in next stitch and every foll. 3rd stitch to last 3 sts. of panel, P3, patt. across 17 sts. of band then * inc. in every 3rd stitch to last 3 sts. of next panel, P3, patt. across 17 sts. of band, Rep. from * to end.

Next Row Work in pattern, starting with Row 3 of cable pattern, until 3 cable rows have been completed, then work Rows 4, 1 and 2 again.

Next Row Decrease 1 stitch in every other cable as follows: *P1, S1, K2, PSSO and knit; P1, S1, K2, PSSO; Rep. from * to last stitch, P1.

Work 1 more row in pattern as now set.

Cast off in pattern. Repeat for remaining three panels.

Sew up final seam as before and small seam on bottom band.

Fold over 16 rows of stocking stitch on waistband and fasten down to bottom of rib on wrong side. Insert 1in Peta-stretch elastic to required length.

Reverting to side seams and eliminating the cable side bands

I mentioned in the introduction that once you have established the correct size panels for your size and shape you can revert to having side seams and eliminate the mock cable side bands. This will give you a conventional style but, most importantly, will fit correctly.

Method Add 1.5in (12 sts.) to each side of the back and front panels, total 24 sts. (this is to compensate for the side bands), then add half the stitches for each of the side panels.

Jumper without cable bands.

Straight armhole When reaching the armhole, cast off the amount of stitches you have added on for the side panels, leaving you an extra 24 sts. for each of the back and front panels. Continue working neckline in normal position, remembering that you will have 12 sts. extra on each of the shoulders.

Shaped armhole When reaching the armhole, cast off half the amount of the underarm cast-off stitches (subtracting 1 stitch for sizes 1, 3 and 5). Decrease every alternate row until the number of stitches for back and front panels, plus 24 sts., remain. Continue working neckline in normal position, remembering that you will have 12 sts. extra on each of the shoulders.

ABOUT THE AUTHOR

Syvia Wynn's innovative approach to knitting and sewing was inspired by visits she made to crofts in the Outer Hebrides in search of Harris Tweed for her garments. She found a weaver who would work designs in specific colours for her, and then ply and scour the same wools for knitting.

Later, living and working in a rural 17th century cottage, her eyes would fall on the wide variety of birds and animals around her, and she began to reproduce them on sweaters using the Swiss darned embroidery technique. These became so popular that she went on to produce embroidery kits for the designs.

Her revolutionary made-to-measure knitwear method was a response to her own change of shape as she grew older – from hour-glass to pear-shaped, as she puts it. Discarding the conventional patterns which increase in size all over, she devised her simple panel-based system which accommodates every size and shape.

Sylvia Wynn gives lectures throughout the country, spreading the message that knitting and sewing should be seen as creative arts which give satisfaction and a sense of achievement. This is her first book.

Index

TITLES AVAILABLE FROM
GMC Publications

BOOKS

UPHOLSTERY

The Upholsterer's Pocket Reference Book	*David James*
Upholstery: A Complete Course (Revised Edition)	*David James*
Upholstery Restoration	*David James*
Upholstery Techniques & Projects	*David James*
Upholstery Tips and Hints	*David James*

TOYMAKING

Scrollsaw Toy Projects	*Ivor Carlyle*
Scrollsaw Toys for All Ages	*Ivor Carlyle*

DOLLS' HOUSES AND MINIATURES

1/12 Scale Character Figures for the Dolls' House	*James Carrington*
Americana in 1/12 Scale: 50 Authentic Projects	*Joanne Ogreenc & Mary Lou Santovec*
Architecture for Dolls' Houses	*Joyce Percival*
The Authentic Georgian Dolls' House	*Brian Long*
A Beginners' Guide to the Dolls' House Hobby	*Jean Nisbett*
Celtic, Medieval and Tudor Wall Hangings in 1/12 Scale Needlepoint	*Sandra Whitehead*
Creating Decorative Fabrics: Projects in 1/12 Scale	*Janet Storey*
The Dolls' House 1/24 Scale: A Complete Introduction	*Jean Nisbett*
Dolls' House Accessories, Fixtures and Fittings	*Andrea Barham*
Dolls' House Furniture: Easy-to-Make Projects in 1/12 Scale	*Freida Gray*
Dolls' House Makeovers	*Jean Nisbett*
Dolls' House Window Treatments	*Eve Harwood*
Easy to Make Dolls' House Accessories	*Andrea Barham*
Edwardian-Style Hand-Knitted Fashion for 1/12 Scale Dolls	*Yvonne Wakefield*
How to Make Your Dolls' House Special: Fresh Ideas for Decorating	*Beryl Armstrong*
Make Your Own Dolls' House Furniture	*Maurice Harper*
Making Dolls' House Furniture	*Patricia King*
Making Georgian Dolls' Houses	*Derek Rowbottom*
Making Miniature Chinese Rugs and Carpets	*Carol Phillipson*
Making Miniature Food and Market Stalls	*Angie Scarr*
Making Miniature Gardens	*Freida Gray*
Making Miniature Oriental Rugs & Carpets	*Meik & Ian McNaughton*

CRAFTS

Making Hand-Sewn Boxes: Techniques and Projects	*Jackie Woolsey*
Making Knitwear Fit	*Pat Ashforth & Steve Plummer*
Making Mini Cards, Gift Tags & Invitations	*Glennis Gilruth*
Making Soft-Bodied Dough Characters	*Patricia Hughes*
Natural Ideas for Christmas: Fantastic Decorations to Make	*Josie Cameron-Ashcroft & Carol Cox*
New Ideas for Crochet: Stylish Projects for the Home	*Darsha Capaldi*
Papercraft Projects for Special Occasions	*Sine Chesterman*
Patchwork for Beginners	*Pauline Brown*
Pyrography Designs	*Norma Gregory*
Pyrography Handbook (Practical Crafts)	*Stephen Poole*
Rose Windows for Quilters	*Angela Besley*
Rubber Stamping with Other Crafts	*Lynne Garner*
Sponge Painting	*Ann Rooney*
Stained Glass: Techniques and Projects	*Mary Shanahan*
Step-by-Step Pyrography Projects for the Solid Point Machine	*Norma Gregory*
Tassel Making for Beginners	*Enid Taylor*
Tatting Collage	*Lindsay Rogers*
Tatting Patterns	*Lyn Morton*
Temari: A Traditional Japanese Embroidery Technique	*Margaret Ludlow*
Trip Around the World: 25 Patchwork, Quilting and Appliqué Projects	*Gail Lawther*
Trompe l'Oeil: Techniques and Projects	*Jan Lee Johnson*
Tudor Treasures to Embroider	*Pamela Warner*
Wax Art	*Hazel Marsh*

MAGAZINES

WOODTURNING • WOODCARVING
FURNITURE & CABINETMAKING • THE ROUTER • WOODWORKING
THE DOLLS' HOUSE MAGAZINE • OUTDOOR PHOTOGRAPHY
BLACK & WHITE PHOTOGRAPHY
MACHINE KNITTING NEWS • BUSINESSMATTERS

The above represents a selection of titles currently published or scheduled to be published.
All are available direct from the publishers or through bookshops, newsagents and specialist retailers.
To place an order, or to obtain a complete catalogue, contact:

GMC Publications,
Castle Place, 166 High Street, Lewes, East Sussex BN7 1XU, United Kingdom
Tel: 01273 488005 Fax: 01273 478606
E-mail: pubs@thegmcgroup.com

Orders by credit card are accepted